Freeman, Sc.

RECEPTION OF CAPTAIN KOTZEBUE AT THE ISLAND OF OTDIA

PREFACE.

THE flattering requisitions of those readers who found amusement in the narrative of my former voyage, independently of its scientific details, form an incentive to my present publication. All mere nautical minutiæ, which might be deemed tedious, with the exception of such as were indispensable, have been omitted. Various contingencies have delayed the appearance of these Volumes; but I still hope they will not have altogether lost the charm of novelty.

With respect to my style, I rely upon the favour formerly shewn me. Devoted from my earliest youth to the sea-service, I have had no leisure for cultivating the art of authorship.

INTRODUCTION.

IN the month of March of the year 1823, I was appointed by his Imperial Majesty Alexander the First, of glorious memory, to the command of a ship, at that time unfinished, but named the Predpriatie (the Enterprise). She had been at first destined for a voyage purely scientific, but circumstances having occurred which rendered it necessary to change the object of the expedition, I was ordered to take in at Kronstadt a cargo to Kamtschatka, and to sail from the latter place to the north-west coast of America, in order to protect the Russian American Company from the smuggling carried on there by foreign traders. On this station my ship was to remain for one year, and then, being relieved by another, to return to Kronstadt. The course to be followed, both in going and returning, was left entirely to my own discretion.

On the first of May, the ship, whose Russian name, Predpriatie, I shall for the future omit, was declared complete. She was the first vessel built in Russia under a roof, (a very excellent plan,) was the size of a frigate of a middling rank, and, that she might not be unnecessarily burdened, was provided with only twenty-four six-pounders.

My crew consisted of Lieutenants Kordinkoff, Korsakoff, Bordoschewitsch, and Pfeifer; the Midshipmen Gekimoff, Alexander von Moller, Golowin, Count Heiden, Tschekin, Murawieff, Wukotitsch, and Paul von Moller; the Mates, Grigorieff, Gekimoff, and Simokoff, eight petty officers, and one hundred and fifteen sailors. We were accompanied by Professors Eschscholz and Lenz as Naturalists; Messrs. Preus and Hoffman as Astronomer and Mineralogist; and Messrs. Victor and von Siegwald as Chaplain and Physician; so that, in all, we reckoned one hundred and forty-five persons.

We were richly stored with astronomical and other scientific instruments: we possessed two pendulum apparatus, and a theodolite made expressly for our expedition by the celebrated Reichenbach. This valuable instrument was executed with wonderful precision, and was of the greatest use in our astronomical observations on shore.

In June the ship arrived at Kronstadt, and on the 14th of July (old style, according to which all reckonings will be made in this voyage,) she lay in the harbour fully equipped and ready to sail. On that day the cannon of the fortress and of the fleet in the roads announced the arrival of the Emperor, whom we had the pleasure of receiving on board our vessel.

His Majesty, after a close examination of the ship, honoured us by the assurance of his imperial satisfaction; the sailors received a sum of money, and I and my officers a written expression of thanks.

With the gracious cordiality peculiar to him, the amiable monarch wished us a happy voyage, and retired followed by our enthusiastic blessings.

We did not then anticipate that we had seen him for the last time. On our return, his lofty spirit had ascended to the regions of bliss: from whence he looks down on his beloved brother, rejoicing to be even surpassed by him in the virtues of a sovereign.

VOYAGE TO BRAZIL.

WE remained in the roads of Kronstadt till the 28th of July, when, after a painful parting from a beloved and affectionate wife, the wind proving favourable, I gave the order to weigh anchor.

The whole crew was in high spirits, and full of hope: the task of weighing anchor and setting sail was executed with alertness and rapidity; and as the ship began her course, cutting the foaming billows, the men joyfully embraced each other, and with loud huzzas expressed their hearty wishes for the success of our undertaking. To me this scene was highly gratifying. Such a disposition in a crew towards an enterprise from which toils and dangers must be anticipated, afforded a satisfactory presumption that their courage and spirits would not fail when they should be really called into exercise. With a good ship and a cheerful crew the success of a voyage is almost certain. We fired a salute of seven guns, in reply to the farewell from the fortress of Kronstadt, and, the wind blowing fresh, soon lost sight of its towers.

As far as Gothland all went well, and nothing disturbed the general cheerfulness; but here a sudden storm from the west attacked us so unexpectedly as scarcely to give time for the necessary precautions. Tossed to and fro by the swelling and boisterous waves, I was not, I must confess, altogether free from anxiety.

With a new and untried ship, and men somewhat out of practice, a first storm is naturally attended by many causes of disquiet not afterwards so seriously felt. In the present instance, however, these untoward circumstances were rather productive of the ludicrous than the terrific; and whatever might be my solicitude as commander, I experienced but little sympathy from my officers. The strength and extent of the motion to which we were about to be exposed had not been duly estimated, and the movable articles in the cabins were generally ill secured. This was particularly the case in the state-cabin, occupied by twenty persons: not a table or a chair would remain in its place; every thing rolling about in its own stupid way, in defiance of all rule and order. The frolicsome young officers were delighted with the confusion; and even our seasick men of science could not refrain from laughter when a well-fed pig, which, disturbed by the inconvenience, had taken refuge on the hatchway, ventured from thence to intrude itself among them by a spring through the open window, and looked around in pitiable amazement on finding that, amidst the general clamour, repose was no more attainable in a state-cabin than in its own humble abode. I was meanwhile occupied in narrowly observing the vessel that was to bear us through so many and long-enduring difficulties. Amidst the conflict of the elements, a commander becomes acquainted with his ship, as in the storms of life we learn duly to appreciate our friends. I weighed the defects of mine against its good qualities, and rejoiced that the latter had greatly the preponderance. She was a friend on whom I might rely in case of need. Such a conviction is necessary to the captain: through it alone can his actions acquire the decision and certainty so indispensable in time of danger, and so essential to success. In the course of four-and-twenty hours the storm abated; a favourable wind again swelled our sails, and we enjoyed it doubly after the little troubles we had undergone. At daybreak on the 8th of August we left the island of Bornholm, and found ourselves surrounded by a Russian fleet cruising under the command of Admiral Crown. This meeting with our countrymen was an agreeable surprise to us: they could carry to our beloved homes the assurance, that thus far at least our voyage had been prosperous. We saluted the Admiral with nine guns, received a similar number in return, and continued our course with full sails.

On the 10th of August we anchored opposite the friendly capital of Denmark, where we received on board the theodolite, which had been prepared for us at Munich by Reichenbach, and sent hither. Before the sun appeared above the horizon on the 12th, we were again under sail, with a good wind and a tranquil sea. The sail along the Danish coast was interesting from its beautiful prospects, and numerous buildings illumined by the morning sun.

We passed the Sound the same day, and entered the Categat. Here we were visited in the night by another violent storm. The sky, pealing with incessant thunder, hung heavy and black above us, and spread a fearful darkness over the sea, broken only by tremendous flashes of lightning. The electric fluid, in large masses of fire, threatened us momentarily with destruction; but thanks be to the strong attractive power of the sea, which forms so good a conductor for ships,—without it we had been lost! In the North Sea our voyage was tedious, from the continuance of contrary winds; and in the English Channel dangerous, from the uninterrupted fog. We however reached Portsmouth roads in safety on the 25th of August.

Since it was my intention to double Cape Horn in the best season, namely January or February, it was necessary to lose no time in England. I therefore hastened to London, and resisting all the allurements offered by the magnificence of the capital, immediately procured my charts, chronometers, and astronomical instruments, and returned on board my ship on the 2nd of September, to be in waiting for the first fair wind. The wind however chose, as it often does, to put our patience to the proof. Its perverseness detained us in the roads till the 6th; and though a temporary change then enabled us to sail, we had scarcely reached Portland point when a strong gale again set in directly in our teeth.

The English Channel, on account of its numerous shallows and strong irregular currents, is at all times dangerous: vessels overtaken there by storms during the night are in imminent peril of wreck, and thus every year are great numbers lost.

I myself, on my former voyage in the Rurik, should have infallibly suffered this fate, had the day dawned only half an hour later. Warned therefore by experience, I resolved not to trust to the chance of the night; and fortunately our English pilot, from whom we had not yet parted, was of the same opinion.—This man, who had grown grey in his employment, and was perfectly acquainted with these waters, advised our immediate return to Portsmouth, and that every effort should be made to reach it before sunset. I therefore had the ship put about, and setting as much sail as the violence of the wind would allow, we fled towards our place of refuge, the storm continually increasing. Although we ran pretty quick, we had scarcely got half-way back, before it became so foggy and dark, that the land, which had hitherto been our guide, was no longer discernible. We could not see three hundred fathoms from the ship. The change in our pilot's countenance showed that our situation had become critical. The little, stout, and hitherto phlegmatic fellow became suddenly animated by a new spirit. His black eyes lightened; he uttered several times the well-known English oath which Figaro declares to be "le fond de la langue," rubbed his bands violently together, and at length exclaimed, "Captain! I should like a glass of grog—Devil take me if I don't bring you safe into Portsmouth yet!" His wish was of course instantly complied with.Strengthened and full of courage, he seized the helm, and our destiny depended on his skill.

It was now barely possible to reach Portsmouth with daylight by taking the shortest way through the Needles, a narrow strait between the Isle of Wight and the mainland, full of shallows, where even in clear weather a good pilot is necessary. The sun was already near setting, when an anxious cry from the watch announced the neighbourhood of land, and in the same instant we all perceived, at about a hundred fathoms' distance, a high fog-enveloped rock, against which the breakers raged furiously.

Our pilot recognised it for the western point of the Isle of Wight at the entrance of the Needles, and the danger we were in only animated his spirits. He seized the helm with both hands, and guiding it with admirable dexterity, the ship flew, amidst the storm, through the narrow and winding channels to which the shallows confined it, often so close upon the impending rocks, that it seemed scarcely possible to pass them without a fatal collision.

A small vessel that had sailed with us for some time at this moment struck, and was instantly swallowed by the waves without a possibility of saving her. This terrible sight, and the consciousness that the next moment might involve us in a similar fate, made every one on board gaze in silent anxiety on the direction we were taking: even the pilot said not a word.

The twilight had nearly given way to total darkness when we reached Portsmouth roads; the joy with which we hailed this haven of safety, and our mutual congratulations on our preservation, may be easily imagined: our pilot now fell back into his former phlegm, and seating himself with a glass of grog by the fireside, received our thanks and praises with equal indifference.

This equinoctial storm raged itself out during the night, and the first rays of the sun again brought us fine weather and a fair wind, which enabled us once more to quit the English harbour. In no situation are the vicissitudes so striking as those experienced at sea. The wind, which had so lately attacked us with irresistible fierceness, was now become too gentle, and we were detained nine days in the Channel by calms, before we could reach the Atlantic Ocean.

Here a fresh north wind occasioned near our track the appearance called a water-spout; which consists of a three-cornered mass of foaming water, with the point towards the sea, and the broad upper surface covered with a black cloud.—We now held a southerly course, and after encountering much rough weather, on the 22nd of September reached the parallel of Lisbon, where we enjoyed the warmer temperature, and congratulated ourselves on having left behind us the region of storms. We steered straight for the island of Teneriffe, where we intended providing ourselves with wine. A fresh trade-wind carried us rapidly and smoothly forward; the whole crew was in fine health and cheered by one of the most beautiful mornings of this climate, when our pleasure in the near prospect of a residence on this charming island was most painfully interrupted by the accident of a sailor falling overboard. The rapidity with which we were driving before the wind frustrated all our efforts to save him, and the poor fellow met his death in the waves. Our cheerfulness was now perfectly destroyed; and my regret for the accident was increased by the fear of the evil impression it might make on the minds of the other men.—Sailors are seldom free from superstition, and if mine should consider this misfortune as a bad omen, it might become such in reality by casting down the spirits so essential in a long and perhaps dangerous voyage. A crew tormenting itself with idle fears will never lend that ready obedience to a commander which is necessary for its own preservation. The messmates of the unfortunate man continued to gaze mournfully towards the spot where he had sunk, till the sight of land, as we sailed about noon past the small rocky island of Salvages, seemed to divert their thoughts from the occurrence; their former cheerfulness gradually returned, and my apprehensions subsided.

This evening the island of Teneriffe became perceptible amidst the mist and clouds which veiled its heights. During the night we reached the high black rocks of lava which form its northern points; and at break of day I determined to tack, in order to run into Santa Cruz, the only place in the island where ships can lie at anchor.

The night was stormy, and the high land occasioned violent gusts of wind from various directions. Towards morning the weather improved, but we found that the current had carried us twenty miles to the south-east. These strong currents are common here in all seasons, and, to vessels not aware of them, may in dark nights produce injurious consequences. Having now passed the northern promontory, we steered southward for the roads of Santa Cruz. The shore here, consisting of high, steep masses of lava, presents a picturesque but desolate and sterile landscape, amidst which the eye seeks in vain for some spot capable of producing the rich wine of Teneriffe. Upon a point of rock about a thousand feet above the level of the sea, we saw a telegraph in full activity, probably announcing our arrival. The town next came in sight, and with its numerous churches, convents, and handsome houses, rising in an amphitheatre up the side of a mountain, would have offered a noble and pleasing prospect to eyes accustomed to the monotony of a sea view, but that the majestic Peak, that giant among mountains, rearing in the background its snow-crowned head 13,278 feet above the level of the sea, now stood clear and cloudless before us, enchaining all our faculties, the effect of its appearance rendered still more striking by the sudden parting of the clouds which had previously concealed it from us. This prodigious conical volcano is from its steepness difficult of access, and the small crater on the summit is so closely surrounded by a wall of lava, that in some places there is scarcely room to stand. He who is bold enough to climb it, however, will find himself rewarded with one of the finest prospects in the world. Immediately beneath him, stretches the entire extent of the Teneriffe, with all its lovely scenery; round it the other nineteen Canary Islands; the eye then glances over an immense expanse of waters, beyond which may be descried in the distance the dark forests of the African coast, and even the yellow stripe which marks the verge of the great Desert. With thoughts full of the enjoyments which awaited us, we approached the town. We planned parties to see the country and climb the Peak; and our scientific associates, holding themselves in readiness to land as soon as the boat could be lowered, already rejoiced over the new treasures of mineralogy and botany of which the island seemed to promise so ample a store: meanwhile we had made the usual signal for a pilot; but having in vain waited his appearance, I resolved, as the road was not altogether unknown to me, to cast anchor without him; when, just as we had made our preparations, a ball from the fortress struck the water not far from the ship. At the same time we perceived that all was bustle on the walls; the cannons were pointed, the matches lighted, and plenty of Spanish balls were ready for our reception. Our government being at peace with Spain, this hostile conduct was quite unintelligible to us; but as I had no desire for a battle, I contented myself with drawing off the ship, and lying to beyond the reach of cannon shot, in the hope that a boat would be sent to us with some explanation of it. After, however, waiting a considerable time in vain, perceiving the continuance of warlike preparations on the walls, we were reluctantly obliged to renounce all hopes of visiting the island or the Peak, and to continue our voyage to Brazil, where we might reckon upon a kinder welcome.

Here, then, was an end to all our promised pleasures. The enrichment of our museum, the merry parties and the choice wine all forfeited to a simple misunderstanding! Whatever might be their motive, it was an inconsiderate action in the Spaniards wantonly to insult the Russian flag; and even if they mistook us for enemies, it was silly to be afraid of a single ship, considering that the renowned Nelson, with an English fleet, had found the fortifications impregnable.

After a few miles' sail we perceived a large three-masted ship endeavouring, with the wind against her, to reach the roads of Santa Cruz. We steered towards her, in hopes that we might obtain some information that should explain the riddle of the treatment we had received. But the ship seemed as much afraid of us as the fortress; and, as soon as she perceived our intention, made all possible haste to avoid us.

It was really laughable enough, but it was also vexatious, that such peaceful people as we were should be considered so terrible. I sent a bullet after the ship, to induce her to stop; she then hoisted the English flag, but never slackened her speed; so that finding we could get no satisfaction, we thought it advisable to take advantage of the fresh trade-wind, to bear away from Teneriffe as quickly as possible. On the following morning we could still see the Peak, a hundred miles off, among the clouds; and we called to mind, as we gazed upon it, the mysterious accounts of its aborigines, of whom it was said, from the resemblance of their teeth to those of grazing animals, that they could only live on vegetables. They embalmed corpses in the manner of the ancient Egyptians, and preserved them in grottoes in the rocks, where they are still to be found. The Spaniards, the first discoverers and appropriators of the island, have described in high terms the state of civilization, methods of agriculture, and remarkably pure morality of these ancient inhabitants, who nevertheless were entirely exterminated by the tyranny and cruelty of their conquerors.

The trade-wind and continued fine weather brought us rapidly on our way towards Brazil. Dolphins, flying-fish, and the large and beautiful gold-fish, called by the Spaniards *bonito*, constantly surrounded the ship, and formed by day a relief from the tedium of gazing on the unvarying billows, as did during the darkness of the night the innumerable phosphorescent animals of the muscle kind, which, studding the black ocean with sparks of fire, produced a dazzling and living illumination. Our naturalist, Professor Eschscholz, has already communicated to the world his microscopical observations upon these marine curiosities.

On the first of October we doubled the Cape Verd Islands, without however seeing the land, which is almost always lost in mist, and steered direct for the Equator. Our progress was now impeded by calms, and the heat began to be oppressive; but care and precaution preserved the crew in perfect health, an effect which strict cleanliness, order, and wholesome diet, will seldom fail to produce, even in long voyages.

At five degrees North latitude, we took advantage of a calm to draw up water from a depth of five hundred fathoms, by means of a machine invented by the celebrated Russian academician Parrot. We found the temperature five degrees by Reaumur, while that of the water on the surface reached twenty-five degrees. To us it appeared ice-cold, and we felt ourselves much refreshed by washing our heads and faces with it. The machine weighed forty pounds, and might contain about a moderate pail-full; but the pressure of the column of water over it was such, that six sailors with a windlass were hardly able to draw it up. We made an attempt to sink it to a thousand fathoms' depth, but the line broke, and we lost the machine; fortunately, however, we were provided with a second.

While we were still more than a hundred miles from land, a swallow alighted on the deck. It is wonderful how far these little animals can fly without resting. At first, it seemed weary, but soon recovered, and flew gaily about. When far out at sea, cut off from every other society than that of our shipmates, any guest from land, even a bird, is welcome. Ours soon became a general favourite, and was so tame, that it would hop on our hands and take the flies we offered him without any symptom of fear. He chose my cabin to sleep in at night; and at sunrise flew again upon deck, where he found every one willing to entertain him, and catch flies for his subsistence. But our hospitality proved fatal to him; he over-ate himself, and died of an indigestion, universally lamented.

On the 11th of October we crossed the Equator at twenty-five degrees W. longitude, reckoning from Greenwich. Having saluted the Southern hemisphere by the firing of guns, our crew proceeded to enact the usual ceremonies. A sailor, who took pride in having frequently passed the Line, directed the performance with much solemnity and decorum. He appeared as Neptune, attired in a manner that was meant to be terribly imposing, accompanied by his consort, seated on a gun-carriage instead of a shell, drawn by negroes, as substitutes for Tritons. In the evening, the sailors represented, amidst general applause, a comedy of their own composition. These sports, while they serve to keep up the spirits of the men, and make them forget the difficulties they have to go through, produce also the most beneficial influence upon their health; a cheerful man being much more capable of resisting a fit of sickness than a melancholy one. It is the duty of commanders to use every innocent means of maintaining this temper in their crews; for in long voyages, when they are several months together wandering on an element not destined by nature for the residence of man, without enjoying even occasionally the recreations of the land, the mind naturally tends to melancholy, which of itself lays the foundation of many diseases, and sometimes even of insanity. Diversion is often the best medicine, and, used as a preservative, seldom fails of its effect.

Below the Equator, we met with a fresh south-east wind, and having also fine weather, we soon reached the coast of Brazil.

RIO JANEIRO.

ON the morning of the 1st of November, consequently in the spring of the Southern hemisphere, we perceived Cape Frio, and in the evening plainly distinguished, by its well-known conical mountain, the entrance to the Bay of Rio Janeiro. A dead calm deprived us of the pleasure of running into the port that night, so that we were compelled to drop our anchor before it; but we found some compensation for our disappointment, in contemplating so much of this charming country as was visible from our ship. The magnificent scenery of Brazil has often been described, but no expression can do justice to its ravishing beauty. Imagination can scarcely picture the exquisite variety of form and colouring of the luxuriant and gigantic vegetation that thickly clothes the valleys and mountains even to the sea-shore. A breeze from the land wafted to us the most delicious perfumes; and crowds of beautiful insects, butterflies, and birds, such as only the tropics produce, hovered about us. Nature seems to have destined these lovely regions for the unmixed enjoyment of her creatures; but, alas! hard labour and a tyrant's whip have, to the unhappy Negro, transformed this Paradise into a place of torment.

The sight of two slave-ships formed a revolting contrast to the enchantment of the prospect: they had that day arrived from Africa, and lay near us at anchor. The trade in human flesh, that foul blot on civilized nations, of which most of them are already ashamed, yet flourishes here in detestable activity, and is carried on, with all the brutality of avarice, under the sanction of the laws. The ships employed in this abominable traffic are so over-crowded that the slaves have scarcely room to move. They are brought up by turns to inhale for a while the refreshing breeze, but the deck being only capable of accommodating a small portion at once, they are soon returned to the confined and pestilential atmosphere below. One third of the human cargo, as a necessary consequence, generally perishes on the voyage, and the remainder reach their place of destination in a state of miserable suffering. The decks of the ships I have just mentioned, were crowded with these unfortunate creatures, naked, fettered, and diseased. Even mothers with infants at their breasts had not been spared by these speculators! What still greater misery might not be concealed beneath the decks!

The darkness, which at once closed from our view all that had delighted and disgusted us, rendered visible an almost incessant flight of rockets, and we heard occasionally, throughout the night, the discharge of guns and musketry from the town. These demonstrations of rejoicing led to the supposition that some important festival was celebrating, or that a great victory had probably been gained; we afterwards learnt, however, that they were occasioned only by the arrest of three ministers, accused of a conspiracy against the Emperor.

At daybreak the chief pilot came on board. This little fat man, proud of his name of Vasco de Gama, which he professed to have inherited in a direct line from the celebrated navigator to the East Indies, was in many respects a good specimen of his countrymen. He was wholly uneducated, as they mostly are; and, next to his ancestry, that in which he took the greatest pride was the independence of Brazil. This feeling, which is general among all classes, enlists each individual personally in support of the existing government, and is its surest guarantee.

Although our pilot had not attained to the renown of his great ancestor, I must do him the justice to say that he understood his business, and guided us very skilfully through the narrow mouth of the Bay. This small entrance, commanded by a fort on a height, is tolerably well secured from the approach of an enemy; and might, by stronger batteries, be made wholly inaccessible, as the channel is so narrow, that a ship in working its way in must always be within half-shot distance. We anchored near the town, among numerous vessels of various nations, and set foot once more on terra-firma, after being fifty-two days at sea since leaving England.

Beautiful as this country always appears to an European eye, it has perhaps no scene so strikingly splendid and picturesque as that which presents itself within this Bay. The rich and novel peculiarity of the landscape is contrasted with the handsome buildings of the town, rising amphitheatrically round the harbour; and these again derive a curious effect from the tall and slender palm-trees, which, thickly interspersed among them, throw their strongly defined and waving shadows upon the white surface of the contiguous houses; and the whole is crowned by the numerous convents which are seen above the town, in the distance, clinging like swallows'-nests, to the precipitous sides of the mountains.

We had hardly reefed our sails, when the Russian Vice-Consul, Von Kielchen, and an officer of the Brazilian government, came on board to congratulate us on our arrival. The latter acquainted me with the order of his Government, that every ship of war coming in should salute the fortress with one-and-twenty guns; and in order to remove all doubt that the compliment was designed for the Brazilian flag, he had brought one which, during the salute, he requested us to hoist at the fore-mast.

New and unprecedented as this order was, from a state not yet acknowledged by our government, I determined, rather than risk any disagreement, to comply with it; and having fired the one-and-twenty guns, received from the fortress a similar number in return. Being very anxious not to lose the favourable season for doubling Cape Horn, I urged the Vice-Consul to expedite as much as possible the delivery of provisions and other necessaries to the ship; for this purpose, however, a delay of four weeks was required, and this time I determined to employ in astronomical observations. M. Von Kielchen procured me for this purpose a convenient country-house, situated on the romantic little bay of Botafogo, of which I took possession on the following day, accompanied by our astronomer, M. Preus; leaving the care of the ship to my officers.

In the supposition that the history of Brazil may not be familiar to every reader, male and female,—for I hope to have many of the latter,—I will preface the narration of my residence here with the following notices.

This great empire in South America, called Brazil, from a wood which grows there in great abundance, resembling in colour a red-hot coal, (in the Portuguese "*Brasa*,") is one of the richest and most fertile countries in the world. It was accidentally discovered in the year 1500, by a Portuguese named Cabral, who with a fleet bound for the East Indies, was thrown on these shores.

The riches of the country being at first unknown, it was used as a place of banishment for criminals; but subsequently, when the convicts began to cultivate the sugar-cane, and the gold and diamond mines were discovered, Brazil acquired a higher value in the eyes of the Portuguese government.

A Viceroy was therefore sent out, with the strongest injunctions to close the Brazilian ports against all foreign powers, in order to preserve to Portugal the exclusive trade in the diamonds and other precious stones with which it was now found that the country abounded. For a long time, this beautiful land, rich in all the gifts of nature, languished under the rule of Portuguese Viceroys, with a thinly-scattered population, poor, oppressed, and destitute of all mental culture. At length, the year 1807 opened to it a brighter prospect. Napoleon's ambitious views extending even to Portugal, forced the Royal Family to take refuge in the colonies. They were followed by fourteen thousand soldiers, and about twelve thousand other adherents. The presence of a court and government in the capital, Rio Janeiro, had the most beneficial influence on all the interests of the country. The ports were opened to all European ships, and commerce, wealth, and civilization advanced rapidly.

Napoleon's victories having found a final termination, in his banishment to St. Helena, the King of Portugal returned, in 1821, to his European dominions, leaving the Regency of Brazil to his son, the Crown Prince, Pedro, already married to an Austrian princess.

But the example of the newly-established republics of America had a powerful effect on the minds of the people; the King's departure was a signal for the breaking out of revolutionary disturbances, which, though the Crown Prince could not appease, he was, nevertheless, by means of a strong party he had gained over, enabled to direct. In the year 1822, he declared Brazil independent of the mother-country,—promised the people a Constitution,—and was at last proclaimed Emperor, by the title of Pedro the First. From the day when the nation tendered its allegiance, the Emperor and all patriots have worn on the left arm a green cockade inscribed with the words, "Independence or Death." At the coronation, the order of the Southern Cross was founded, and the new national flag hoisted: it is green, with a yellow square in the middle, on which is represented the Earth, surrounded by thirteen stars (the number of the provinces), and leaves of coffee and tobacco, as the produce of the country.

The government, at the time of our residence in Brazil, was nothing less than constitutional. This is sufficiently proved by the tumultuary arrest of the above-mentioned three Ministers, by the arbitrary dispersion of the Deputies from the provinces, called together expressly to form a Constitutional Assembly, and by the expression of the Emperor, that he required unconditional submission, even if he should choose, like Charles the Twelfth, to send his boot to them as his representative. It is possible that the Emperor has been in some measure forced to these violent proceedings by the contentions of the various parties, each of which seeks its own interest without concerning itself about the general welfare. His personal character is much praised.

A captain of one of the Russian-American Company's ships, who had been in Rio Janeiro, related to me the following anecdote of his benevolence. Two sailors belonging to his crew had been ashore, and having got drunk, were found lying senseless on the road to Corcovado. The Emperor and Empress happening to ride that way, attended only by a few servants, saw them, and supposed them to be sick. The Emperor immediately dismounted, rubbed their temples with his own hand, and endeavoured to restore them to their senses, but in vain. He then sent for his own surgeon, and dispatched them under his care to the hospital, from whence on the following morning, having slept off their intoxication, they were dismissed as cured.—Another, and a different anecdote, I heard from a painter from Vienna, who was residing in Rio Janeiro. The Emperor, wishing to have a whole-length portrait of himself, sent for the painter to place his easel in a room in the palace, and commenced sitting. The first outline was scarcely made, when an officer, whose business it was to report the arrival of ships, entered with the list. The names of the ships and captains, of various nations and languages with which the officer was unacquainted, puzzled him, and he read so stammeringly, and sometimes almost unintelligibly, that the Emperor, enraged at his ignorance, seized a stick, and the officer, only by a rapid flight round the easel, in which he was at first pursued by the monarch, escaped the intended chastisement. We shall be less surprised at this conduct, if we consider the point of civilization to which the country had attained when this Prince first seized the helm. May he succeed in elevating it to what his government may make it,—the happiest, as well as the loveliest and most fruitful empire in the world!

The Brazilian fleet, then commanded by the celebrated Lord Cochrane, consisted of one ship of the line, two frigates, three brigs, and some smaller vessels. Inconsiderable as was this force, it was in good order, and under the direction of its skilful and heroic commander, had done wonders. Lord Cochrane had recently, with his single ship of the line and one frigate only, attacked and defeated a Portuguese squadron of two ships of the line and four frigates, pursued them to the port of Lisbon, and made prize of forty merchant vessels they were convoying. For this exploit, he received from the Emperor the appointment of Grand Admiral, and the title of Marquis of Marenham, after one of the provinces. He had before served the republic of Chili; and, it is said, in the midst of his warlike ardour, he had not forgotten the care of his private finances.

This was his first year in the Brazilian service. I was curious to see so celebrated a man, and soon found an opportunity of forming an acquaintance with him, which led to a frequent intercourse. His external deportment is repulsive rather than attractive; he is somewhat taciturn; and it is difficult, in ordinary conversation, to discover the intelligence and information which he really possesses. He is turned of fifty years of age, tall and thin: his attitude is stooping, his hair red, his features strongly marked, and the expression of his countenance serious: his sparkling, lively eyes, concealed by overhanging eyebrows, are generally fixed on the ground, and seldom even raised to the person he is addressing. His lady forms a striking contrast with him: she is young, handsome, lively in conversation, extremely amiable, and so devotedly attached to him, that she exposes her life to the greatest danger rather than leave his side, and has remained in his ship during all his battles in the South American service.

Cochrane frequently expressed to me a wish to enter the Russian service, in order to assist the Greeks, and fight the Turks. This object he has since attained by other means. War appears to be an indispensable necessity to his nature; and a dangerous struggle in a just cause is his highest enjoyment. How this enthusiasm can be united to the great love of money of which he is accused, it is not easy to imagine.

My short residence in Brazil passed rapidly and agreeably in my necessary occupations, and the enjoyment of the charming environs of my country-house. The effect which so total a change of climate and scenery produces on European spirits, even when not experienced for the first time, is really astonishing. The eye can fix on no one object which is not directly the reverse of any thing to which it has been accustomed. The birds, insects, trees, flowers, all wear a foreign aspect, even to the blades of grass. By its strange forms and colourings, but especially by its overflowing abundance, all nature here demands attention. Throughout the day, myriads of the most beautiful butterflies, beetles, and humming-birds, display their various colours in the sun, which has scarcely set, before innumerable swarms of fire-flies illuminate the scene. I had seldom time for excursions; therefore, as it usually happens to sailors, I can say little of the interior.

Botafogo, where, on account of the salubrity of the air, the richest and most distinguished of the inhabitants of Rio Janeiro have fixed their country-houses, is the most attractive spot in the immediate environs of the capital. Among the mountains which form the background of the view from the Bay, is one solid rock, very remarkable from the resemblance of its figure to an enormous church-steeple; it rises, according to a geometrical admeasurement of our scientific companion Lenz, to the height of fifteen hundred and eighty feet above the level of the sea. With infinite pains, a road has been conducted to the summit, where the space is so confined that a few persons only can be accommodated at the same time, but from whence the prospect is indescribably magnificent: it is called Corcovado, and is a favourite ride with the Emperor.

From Botafogo the road to the capital is studded on both sides with pretty villas. The town derives its name, Rio Janeiro, or January river, from an error on the first discovery of the bay, which, owing to the narrowness of its mouth, was mistaken for a river, and named after the current month. Its interior by no means corresponds with its handsome appearance from the bay, the streets being narrow and dirty, and the buildings very tasteless. Clumsy churches and convents are found in plenty, but there is little worthy the attention of the traveller, except the Museum, which has a rich collection of rare natural curiosities, and valuable minerals. The extent of the town is considerable, and it contains about two hundred and fifty thousand inhabitants, of which however two-thirds are negroes, and the rest principally mulattoes and other people of colour. A white face is seldom to be seen in the streets; but the blacks are so numerous, that one might fancy oneself in Africa.

Among these are a few free men; but the greater part are slaves degraded to beasts of burden. The immense weights they carry are usually fastened on a plank, each end of which is borne by a negro, keeping time to his steps by a monotonous and melancholy song in his native language, and goaded by the whip to renewed efforts, when the failing of his voice indicates almost utter exhaustion. They often carry heavily laden baskets on their heads; and even women are not exempt from this labour.

On Sundays and holidays they also sing in time to their steps, as they stroll about, but the tune has a more lively character; and they sometimes accompany their voices on a little instrument composed of a few steel springs. They understand no other language than that of their distant country, and therefore, though the ceremony of baptism is never omitted, they receive no instruction in the doctrines of Christianity; thus, while an appearance of anxiety concerning the salvation of their souls is maintained, they continue sunk in the state of misery and darkness which hopeless bodily suffering is so calculated to produce. The few free blacks are either manumitted slaves or their descendants: they are mostly mechanics engaged in trade. The mulattoes are generally of illegitimate birth, but are sometimes the offspring of marriages between blacks and the lowest class of whites. From their connexion with blacks or whites spring all the various gradations of colour met with among the inhabitants of Brazil. The mulattoes and free negroes form the middle classes; the few whites found among them being the worst of characters, ignorant and vicious to the last degree; their repulsive exterior is worthy of their abandoned lives: they are usually *retail* slave dealers, and keep shops where these miserable beings are exposed to view, and may be examined and purchased like any other ware. About twenty thousand negroes are annually brought to Brazil; the average price of a female is three hundred, and of a man six hundred piastres.

The principal food of the negroes is a sort of thick paste called Manioc, which is prepared from Tapioca by kneading in hot water; to an European palate it has a disagreeable flavour, but may be nutritious, as the slaves mostly look well-fed; I doubt, however, its being wholesome without a mixture of other food, and I even think it possible that it may be the original cause of a terrible disease to which the negroes alone are subject, and of which they know nothing in their own country. Large tumours appear on their faces and legs, which do not break, but increase in size till in some of the sufferers the human form can scarcely be recognised. A convent situated on a little island, called Dos Fradres, in the bay of Rio Janeiro, and not far from the town, contains a hospital, under the superintendence of the government, for sick negro slaves. I have not been able to learn whether this disease has been successfully treated here. The father of the Emperor, while he remained in Rio Janeiro, often visited the convent; and a room is shown where he used to take refuge when it thundered, as he was excessively fearful in a storm, and, from some unknown cause, esteemed this chamber peculiarly safe.

On the 19th of November, the celebration of the anniversary of the coronation, and the establishment of the Order of the Southern Cross, attracted me to the capital.

It was scarcely daybreak when the thunder of the cannon from all the batteries, and from the ships in the roads, recalled the remembrance of this happy event, which had taken place only the preceding year. The streets were filled with people; soldiers in their dress-regimentals hastened to their various places of rendezvous; and the negroes, released from labour, formed a part of the cheerful throng. At eleven o'clock, the Emperor and Empress, in a magnificent carriage drawn by eight horses, and escorted by a troop of guards in handsome uniforms, arrived at the principal church. A number of carriages, containing the suite of the Imperial pair, followed, all at a slow pace, that the people might have more time to enjoy the spectacle.

At some distance from the door, the Emperor and Empress alighted, and entered the church in procession, surrounded by the Knights of the Southern Cross; they were met by the Bishop and the whole body of the clergy, and conducted with great pomp to a throne erected at the right side of the altar, which the Emperor ascended, while his consort took her place in a pew on the left. After the service, performed by a good choir to excellent music, the Bishop came forward and delivered a very long discourse, descriptive of the various virtues of the Emperor, comparing him to Peter the Great of Russia, and pointing out how he ought to administer the government for the good of his subjects. The comparison he was pleased to institute between the monarch and his illustrious namesake is only so far just,.as, in the uncultivated state of the two nations, both have had similar materials to work upon. Whether Don Pedro, with much greater means, will effect as much as our immortal Peter, time will show. One of the hopes of Brazil is already extinguished by the death of the Empress, who in a short time had done much for science and the arts. When the sermon was over, their Majesties returned to the Palace, amidst an uninterrupted firing of cannon. They then received the congratulations of the court, and at four o'clock the Emperor reviewed in the great market-place, where a temple was erected for the imperial family, a body of four thousand five hundred troops, formed in a half circle round the temple. In their venerable commander, Don José de Currado, a field-marshal, of eighty years of age, I joyfully recognised the former governor of St. Katharine's, who, on my first voyage round the world, under the command of the present Admiral Krusenstein, received me so hospitably. The observations I had an opportunity of making upon the soldiers, before the arrival of the Emperor, were not altogether unfavourable; though, it must be confessed, the good people seemed to have no very high notion of discipline; smoking, and all kinds of irregularities, being permitted even in the front ranks. Their uniform was handsome and suitable; that of the musicians chiefly attracted my attention. Every colonel of a regiment has the right of dressing his band according to his fancy; and as tastes are very various, so of course are these costumes, though the Asiatic predominates; some being attired as Turks, others as Indians. In one regiment, indeed, a quantity of coloured feathers, worn on the head and round the body, formed the only covering.

As soon as the Emperor and Empress, both on horseback and surrounded by a splendid court, were seen in the distance, the cannon sent forth its loudest roar, the soldiers threw away their cigars, the multitude waved their hats, the ladies in the balconies their white pocket-handkerchiefs, and all shouted "Viva l'Emperador." The cortège approached slowly; the Emperor, from the superior richness of his uniform, glittering amidst the splendid throng, like Syrius in the starry sky. His colossal figure seemed literally covered with gold lace; his breast sparkled with diamonds, and his strong features were shaded by a hat richly decorated with jewels. The Express was more tastefully attired in a simple black riding-dress, embroidered with gold. When she had taken her place in the temple, his Majesty assumed the command of the troops and paraded them before her. As soon as his powerful voice was heard, the thunder of the cannon again burst forth; the Turks, Indians, and above-mentioned Popinjays, blew their trumpets, while the shout from the people of "Viva l'Emperador" was loudest amidst the uproar. The columns of the military having several times defiled before the Empress, the parade terminated, and the Imperial family and their court repaired to the theatre. I had been seated in my box a few minutes before they entered the building, which was suffocatingly full, and I was surprised to find it as good in its architecture and arrangements as the generality of European theatres. The boxes were occupied by whites only, and many female faces were there to be seen as fair as those of Northern Europe; the tender red of the youthful cheek, the bright, black eye and jetty hair increased the attraction of these brilliant complexions; but many of the ladies have brown, and even very light hair. Their dress was tastefully arranged in the Parisian fashion: the art of the toilet appears indeed to be the only one they study, as their education does not always proceed so far as reading and writing, although they are not deficient in natural capabilities; their conversation is often as graceful and piquant as that of European ladies. Nor is general information much more extended among the gentlemen, as the following anecdote will testify. When, in 1817, the Russian frigate Kamschatka anchored in the Port of Rio Janeiro, it was visited by many Brazilians of rank, and amongst others by an officer who expressed much surprise at finding a crucifix in the cabin. He knew, indeed, that the Russians professed the Greek religion, but was wholly ignorant that this church formed any part of the Christian community.

It is the custom here to pay visits in the theatre, which are indeed more highly prized than those made at their houses, as the attention is more publicly manifested. On these occasions the animated intercourse between the young people of the different sexes is frequently accompanied by glances sufficiently expressive to betray its object.

The pit presented a very singular appearance, from its assemblage of various complexions, including every possible shade from black to white, although the darker tints had greatly the preponderance. Nor was the distinction of manners among the different portions of the audience less striking. No theatre in Europe can boast of more decorum and politeness than prevails here in the boxes; but the noisy and coarse vulgarity of the pit would not be tolerated in a more refined nation. All eyes were eagerly directed towards the Imperial box, when its curtain, which before had been close drawn, was thrown open; their Majesties then appeared standing in the front, the back of the box being filled by Knights of the Southern Cross. Hats and handkerchiefs were now again waved, and on every side resounded "Viva l'Emperador, l'Emperadriza, la Monarchia!" This enthusiasm having been rewarded by gracious acknowledgments, the drop curtain rose, and an actress came forward to recite a prologue in praise of the Emperor. Then followed a piece of which I understood very little; and the whole was concluded by a ballet, greatly superior to my expectations. During the performance, the Emperor gave audience in his box to many of his subjects, the interview always beginning with the homage of kissing hands on the bended knee. As soon as the curtain rose, the company in the pit became tolerably quiet, and much more attentive than those in the boxes; the latter appearing to take more interest in conversation with their acquaintances than in the performance. I paid my respects to Lord Cochrane and his amiable wife in their box, and remained with them till the conclusion of the piece.

He spoke much of Chili, and wore even on this day of ceremony, a Chilian uniform and a blue scarf, its honorary decoration. This surprised me the more, as he seemed dissatisfied with the Chilian government. His explanation was, that the Emperor had not yet decided what his Brazilian uniform should be, and consequently, that he was still obliged to wear that of Chili. The lady preferred Chili to Brazil, and believed that the heat of this climate did not agree with her health.

On the 27th of November, all our stores being laid in, bidding a cordial farewell to Brazil, I returned to my ship, intending to continue our voyage on the following day. Accordingly at five o'clock on the morning of the 28th we spread our sails, and the ebb-tide and a light breeze from the North, bore us slowly from this lovely coast. The wind soon slackened; and we should have been greatly embarrassed but for a number of boats sent by the English squadron, then lying in the roads, to tow us out to sea, by which seasonable assistance we were enabled to clear the bay before evening. The heat of Brazil had not injured the health of our crew. Fresh provisions, much fruit and vegetables, good lemonade instead of the ordinary drink, and a sea bath every evening, were the means I employed for the prevention of sickness. The men were in the best spirits for encountering the storms of the Southern ocean; and I destined the port of Conception, on the coast of Chili, for a resting-place, after having surmounted the difficulties of doubling Cape Horn.

The result of our repeated observations on land, are as follows:—

Latitude of Botafogo	21° 56' 5" South.
Medium Longitude from various observations	43° 7' 32" West.

Every longitude which is given in the course of this voyage is reckoned by the distance from Greenwich, going from West to East. The variation of the needle amounted to 3° East, its inclination to 9° 28'. As the longitude of Cape Frio has been variously laid down, I took much pains to ascertain it exactly. By a very good chronometer, I found the difference between Cape Frio and Botafogo 1° 6' 20"; so that the true longitude of Cape Frio from Greenwich must be 42° 1' 12".

DOUBLING OF CAPE HORN,

AND

RESIDENCE IN CHILI.

WE continued our course to the South very agreeably, with fine weather and a favourable wind. Under thirty-nine degrees of latitude, however, we could already perceive how much further the South pole extends its unfavourable influence than the North. The sky was no longer clear, the wind became changeable and violent, the air much colder, and the frequent sight of the whale, and of a giant bird called the albatross, warned us that we were approaching the stormy region. We afterwards shot one of these birds on the coast of Chili, which measured twelve feet across the wings.

In the parallel of Rio de la Plata, although two hundred miles from land, we were daily carried by the current thirty-nine miles out of our course towards the south-west; so great is the influence of this mighty river at the distance of two hundred and forty miles from its mouth.

On the 15th of December, in the beginning of the southern summer, under forty-seven degrees of latitude, where, if the temperature of both hemispheres were equal, the climate would have been that of the South of Germany, or the middle of France, we were overtaken by a violent storm, accompanied by hail and snow. It began from the south-west, but the wind, in the course of twenty-four hours, veered the whole round of the compass, and raised such high and furious billows, that our escape from destruction afforded ample proof, notwithstanding a considerable leak, of our ship's strength, and her architect's skill. From this time we continued our voyage with a fair wind and serene weather.

Between Falkland Islands and the west of Patagonia, we saw great numbers of storm-birds, betokening the neighbourhood of land, and we sailed within speaking distance of a North-American whaler. The dirty ship, and the crew smeared with blubber, had indeed a disgusting appearance; but if we consider to what toils and dangers these poor men are exposed during their voyages, which commonly last several years, in the most tempestuous seas, sometimes sailing about for months without seeing a fish, and suffering in the meanwhile from the want of wholesome food, yet pursuing their object with invincible perseverance, it is impossible to deny them compassion, and even commendation. The North Americans display an industry and perseverance in their commercial undertakings, which is not exceeded even by the English: they are to be met with upon every sea, and in the most unfrequented regions, disdaining nothing, however trivial, from which they can derive profit. On the north-west coast of America, they barter with the savages all kinds of European trifles for the beautiful skin of the sea-otter, which they sell for a high price in China. Many of their vessels take in cargoes of sandal-wood in the South-Sea Islands, for which they also find a good market in China, where it is in great estimation; others pursue the spermaceti whale in the neighbourhood of Cape Horn, and carry on an important traffic in this article.

On the morning of the 23rd of December, we saw in the distance the snow-covered points of the mountains in the dreaded Staten-land. A fresh breeze carried us so near to this inhospitable and desolate island, that we could plainly distinguish the objects on it, even without a telescope. What a contrast to the beauty of Brazil! There nature seems inexhaustible in her splendour and variety; here she has sparingly allowed a thin clothing of moss to the lofty masses of black rock. Seldom do the sun's rays lighten this or the neighbouring island of Terra del Fuego. Vegetation is so blasted by the perpetual cold and fogs, that a few miserable stunted trees can scarcely find subsistence at the foot of the mountains. The sea-birds avoid these barren shores; the very insects disdain them; the dog, the faithful companion of man, and man himself, the inhabitant of every climate under heaven, can alone exist in this; but the warmth of the sun is essential to the development of his faculties. Here he is a mere animal, and of disgusting appearance; small, ill-shaped, with dirty copper-coloured skin, black bristly hair, and devoid of beard. He inhabits a miserable hut made of boughs covered with dried rushes, and appeases his hunger on the raw and often half-decayed flesh of the sea animals, whose skins furnish him with a scanty covering: this is the utmost extent to which his invention has yet led him, in providing defences against the roughness of the climate; and the dreariness of his existence is still unenlivened by any notion of amusement. Yet is this benumbing country situated in the same degree of southern latitude in which in the northern lies my beloved Esthonia, where every comfort of civilization may be enjoyed—the land of my birth, where in the charming form of woman is "garnered up" the happiness of my life, and where I hope to rest at last in the haven of friendship and love, till I set out on that final voyage from which I shall never return.

We had so little wind, that we were only able on the following morning to double the eastern promontory of Staten-land, Cape John; which our chronometers fixed, almost precisely, in the same longitude assigned to it by Captain Cook. I now steered a westerly course along the south coast of Staten-land, contrary to the usual practice of navigators, who run from hence to 60 degrees South, expecting in that latitude to meet with fewer impediments to their passage into the South Sea. Experience has taught me, moreover, that Cape Horn may be doubled with least loss of time by keeping near land, where in the summer months good east winds will often blow, when westerly winds prevail at a distance of forty miles to sea-ward. When we had passed Staten-land, the Terra del Fuego lay in equally fearful form to our right. We continued our course with a moderate north-east wind, and remarked a strong current to the north.

On the noon of the following day we perceived the terrible Cape Horn at a distance of twenty-five miles, lying in the form of a high, round mountain before us. A calm, of which we took advantage to shoot some albatrosses, delayed us for a few hours; but on Christmas-day we doubled the Cape without the slightest difficulty. In the evening, after sailing close alongside the little rocky island of Diego Ramirez, inhabited by immense numbers of sea-birds, we found ourselves in the South Sea. A favourable east wind swelling our sails, on the 28th of December, we did our best to clear the island of Terra del Fuego, before a west wind should impede our progress; but in this we were disappointed, for a sudden storm drove us out of our course to latitude 59½°. Here, for a New Year's gift, we fell in with a fresh south wind, which helped us forward at the rate of eleven miles an hour, and continued to swell our sails, till on the 5th we lost sight of the Terra del Fuego, and joyfully continued our voyage northwards. At Cape Horn, Reaumur's thermometer stood at four degrees; a temperature rendered very disagreeable by our having so recently suffered from oppressive heat. We now hailed with renewed enjoyment the daily increasing warmth.

My sailors had heard much of the dreadful storms which raged at all seasons round Cape Horn, and destroyed so many ships. One of them had recently read to his messmates the history of Lord Anson's unfortunate voyage: they were therefore not quite free from apprehension on approaching this dangerous point, and were agreeably surprised at passing it so quietly. In their joy they hit on the proud, poetical idea, that the very elements themselves respected the Russian flag. This bold imagination took such possession of their minds, that, in the elevation of their spirits, they resolved to represent it in a pantomime, to which I willingly assented, as my own cheerfulness greatly depended on theirs. Accordingly, a throne was erected on the capstan, adorned with coloured flags and streamers, which we were to take for the extreme point of Cape Horn, upon which, shrouded in red drapery, with all becoming dignity and seriousness of aspect, sat the hitherto unknown God Horn, (begotten and born of the sailors' fancy,) the tremendous ruler of the winds and waves in this tempestuous ocean. In his strong right hand he held a large three-pronged oven fork, and in his left a telescope, with which he surveyed the watery expanse seeking for a sacrifice. A grey beard smeared with tar, hung down to his knees, and, probably as a symbol of his marine dominion, instead of a crown, his head was decorated by a leathern pail. Before him lay a large open book, and a pen was stuck behind his ear, to write down the names of the ships which sailed by. The exact purpose of this I could not understand, but the effect was equally good. Upon the lower step of the throne stood two full-cheeked sailors, very much painted, holding bellows, to represent the Winds ready to produce a raging whirlwind at the nod of their ruler. The God seemed in a very ill humour, till at the appearance of a three-masted ship, made of some planks nailed together, his visage suddenly cleared. The crew of the vessel, which was in full sail, pointed to the Cape, and appeared to rejoice in the expectation of doubling it safely. Then did the God Horn give the ominous nod, and the bellows began to work. The ship took in her sails with all possible expedition, but was nevertheless terribly tossed about. The crew, in danger of perishing, offered their supplications to the God, who at length relenting, commanded the winds to subside, and suffered the vessel to pass on in safety. Soon after another vessel appeared bearing our flag, which the God no sooner perceived than he descended from his throne, took the pail respectfully from his head, and made a profound obeisance, in token of homage to the Russian flag. The Æolian attendants blew the gentlest gales, and we soon vanished with out-stretched sails behind our own main-mast. The piece concluded amidst universal applause, and a double portion of grog served to increase the general cheerfulness.

Thus opened the year 1824.—The crew believed that, with the passage of Cape Horn, the greatest danger of the voyage was over, and were full of life and spirits. On the 15th of January we saw far off the Island of St. Maria, and on the following morning knew, by the two high mountains called Biobio's Bosom, from the river which flows between them, that we were approaching the Bay of Conception. As soon as these hills are clearly distinguished, the entrance to the bay is easily found.—In fine weather they are excellent guides.

A brisk south wind carried us swiftly towards the land, which, far from charming the eye with the picturesque beauty of Brazil, presents an almost undeviating straight line.—The round sides of the mountains are but sparingly covered with vegetation, and in this dry season had a sterile appearance. At noon, having doubled the Island of Quiquirino, at the the mouth of the bay, we found ourselves in a smooth and spacious sheet of water, surrounded by crowds of sea-dogs, dolphins, whales, and water-birds, which abound on the coasts of Chili. This part of the country is but thinly inhabited, and a few poor and scattered huts only are visible. During the centuries that it has been in possession of the Spaniards, it has advanced as little as their other colonies in cultivation or civilization.

The calm made it impossible on that day to reach the village of Talcaguana, where ships usually lie at anchor, and we were consequently obliged in the evening to lay-to at some miles distance.

At twelve o'clock at night, the watch on deck observed a large boat approaching with caution to within reach of musket-shot. This slinking about in the dark had a suspicious appearance, especially as the colony having revolted against the mother-country, was in a state of war. Want of light prevented our learning the strength of the boat's crew, or what arms it carried; but we prepared to repel an attack, in which, however, it was manifest the advantage would be greatly on our side. I ordered the watch to hail the boat, which in return addressed us through a trumpet, first in Spanish, and immediately afterwards in English, inquiring to what nation we belonged, and whence, and for what purpose, we were come. Upon our reply that we were Russians and good friends, the boat came nearer, and an officer, well armed with sword and pistols, came on deck, but was so alarmed on perceiving our state of warlike preparations, that he did not utter a word till he had satisfied himself that we were really Russians, and had no hostile intentions.

The cause of his fear lay in the report of a Spanish frigate having been seen cruising on the coast. This officer was an Englishman, in the service of the republic of Chili, and lieutenant of a corvette lying before Talcaguana. He left us with a request, (which was immediately complied with,) that we would hoist a lantern at our fore-mast, as a signal of peace to the inhabitants of Talcaguana, among whom our appearance had spread the greatest anxiety.

Early in the morning I sent an officer ashore to notify our arrival in proper form to the commandant of the place, and to request his permission to furnish ourselves with water and fresh provisions, which was granted in the most courteous manner possible.

Sure of a favourable reception, I immediately weighed anchor, and, having a good wind, dropped it again at noon, at the distance of a musket-shot from Talcaguana, in a depth of five and a half fathoms, after having been fifty days on the voyage from Rio Janeiro, during the whole of which time the crew had enjoyed the most perfect health. Besides our own ship, and the above-mentioned corvette, commanded by Captain Simson, three merchant ships under Chilian, and three whalers under English colours also lay here. In the afternoon I went ashore myself, and paid the Commandant a visit; I was received in the most friendly manner, but with a good deal of Spanish etiquette, by an old man, who was evidently a zealous republican.

He told me, that the first President of the Republic, Freire, whose authority, he gave me to understand, would be very instrumental in furthering his efforts to assist us, was at that moment in the town of Conception. Thither, therefore, I determined to proceed, hoping to see the President, and procure from him a written order for our accommodation.

And here, though it interrupt the course of my narrative, I apprehend some particulars concerning this country may be agreeable to such of my readers as are strangers to it.

The fruitful Chili is a long and narrow strip of coast-land, bathed on the West by the Great Ocean, so falsely called the Pacific; divided on the North from Peru by the desert tract of Atacoma; and on the East, from Buenos Ayres, by the chain of the Cordilleras, or Andes, whose snow-covered summits are diversified by the columns of fire continually emitted from numerous volcanoes; on the South it extends as far as the Straits of Magellan, and indeed also claims the wholly useless island of Terra del Fuego, which is rarely, if ever, visited by a Chilian.

The Spaniard Valdivia may be considered as the real discoverer of Chili. He established here the first Spanish settlement, the present capital, St. Jago, and subsequently, the town of Conception. For a long time the Spaniards were engaged in bloody and uninterrupted war with the original inhabitants of the country, called Araucanians. This strong and enterprising people withdrew into the mountains, where they were invincible, and from whence they have continued, to the present day, to annoy the descendants of the intruders, who acknowledge and have hitherto respected their independence. They still preserve in their mountains and fastnesses their ancient mode of living, and remain faithful to the religion and manners of their ancestors. Unluckily for the Spaniards, they have become very dangerous neighbours by providing themselves with horses, which, as they are skilful riders, enable them to execute their predatory expeditions with a rapidity that renders them almost always successful. A few of them have settled in the valleys, at the foot of the mountains, and adopted the Christian religion, without however amalgamating with the Spaniards, or losing their freedom.

The lower class of the present inhabitants of Chili is a mixed race, sprung from the union of Spaniards with Araucanian women: they are well grown, of a dark brown complexion, and have a lively red in their cheeks. The men are all good riders, and have brought to great perfection the art of catching wild animals with the *lasso*. The upper classes have preserved their Spanish blood pure: they are also very well formed, the females nearly always handsome, and some of them remarkably beautiful. La Pérouse found them decorated with metal rings; they now adorn themselves with much taste in

Parisian fashions, which reach them by the way of Peru: their manners, though they do not approach so nearly to the forms of European society as do those of the upper ranks in Rio Janeiro, are nevertheless not deficient in refinement.

The climate resembles that of the middle of France, and vegetation thrives abundantly in its fertile soil. Among many kinds of native animals, the wild goats are the most numerous, and are scarcely ever tamed. Chili is particularly rich in beautiful birds; troops of parrots are seen on the wing; humming-birds, and butterflies of all kinds, hover round the flowers, and swarms of lantern-flies sparkle through the night; while venomous insects and snakes are unknown.

This fine country has been long neglected. Spanish jealousy allowed no trade with foreign nations; and the introduction of the Inquisition was sufficient to prevent all mental advancement. The inhabitants are also justly accused of idleness, in not having taken more advantage of the productiveness of their soil. Now, however, that they have thrown off the yoke under which their industry was oppressed, and burst the fetters of the Inquisition, which bowed down their minds, they begin to be ashamed of the low grade of civilization on which they stand, in comparison with other nations, and are exerting themselves to attain a more respectable station in the scale.

The Chilians are chiefly indebted for their independence to the well-known General San Martin. In the year 1817, he made the celebrated campaign over the Andes from Buenos Ayres, attacked and completely defeated the Spaniards, and laid the foundation of the freedom of Chili. It is now governed by plenipotentiaries from all the provinces, under the presidency of General Freire.

The Bay of Conception is a most eligible resting-place for the voyager in these seas to touch at, on account of its safe and commodious harbour, its abundant supply of provisions, and the healthiness of its climate. Evidently destined by nature for the central point of Chilian commerce, it must certainly supersede the unsafe roads of Valparaiso. Freire has already determined to establish an Admiralty in the neighbourhood of Talcaguana, and as much as possible to encourage the population of that part of the country. The village of Talcaguana, consisting of about fifty small and poor houses, and another still smaller, called Pencu, have been the only settlements on this bay since the destruction, in the year 1751, of the old town of Conception by an earthquake—no uncommon occurrence in these regions. The new town of this name has been built farther inland, on the banks of the beautiful river Biobio, and is seven miles distant from Talcaguana.

Early in the morning on the 18th of January, I went with Dr. Eschscholtz to Talcaguana, where horses were in waiting to take us to Conception. The heavy, clumsy cars drawn by oxen, which I believe I described in my former voyage, are the only kind of carriage known here; and as even the ladies use these only on state occasions, they perform all their journeys, as in days of old, on horseback.

The Russian flag having waved here but twice since the foundation of the world, curiosity had brought a great crowd to witness my disembarkation; and as it was now ascertained that the Captain was the same who, eight years before, had so much delighted the inhabitants with a ball, many of my old acquaintances and guests had assembled to welcome me. I could not resist their kind and pressing invitations to visit them once more, before going to Conception. I was received with the greatest cordiality, and all possible pains were taken to entertain me; but they complained sadly of the ravages of war, which had brought its usual concomitants, poverty and ruin, in its train. A melancholy change had taken place since my former visit; some of the wealthiest families had removed from Lima, and a striking difference was perceptible in the establishments of those that remained; while the silver utensils which formerly had been so common even among the poorer inhabitants, had wholly disappeared, and were replaced by a bad description of stone ware.

The same traces of desolation were visible along the once beautiful road to Conception, whither we proceeded on spirited horses, as soon as we had paid the required visits. Instead of the numerous flocks and herds which once adorned the meadows, burnt villages, uncultivated fields, devastated orchards, and swarms of beggars, presented a painful picture of universal want and misery. Such are the heavy sacrifices with which Chili has purchased her independence. May she enjoy their fruits under a government sufficiently wise and powerful to restore her prosperity!

Our two hours' ride afforded ample time and scope for these reflections; and on reaching the town, we were concerned to find similar symptoms of misfortune. A great part of it lay in ruins; and the houses yet standing were occupied, not by useful citizens, or active, speculating merchants, but by soldiers. The former have, with few exceptions, withdrawn from Conception to Mexico and Peru. But the war of the Revolution is not chargeable with all the desolation which has befallen this unhappy town. A year before it broke out, a great horde of wild Araucanians, availing themselves of an opportunity when the Chilian troops were elsewhere employed, fell so suddenly upon the town during the night, that the inhabitants, who had not the slightest warning till the enemy was within their walls, were unable to defend themselves. Well knowing that they could not maintain their post, the Araucanians were active in the work of rapine and murder, and at length withdrew to their mountains laden with rich booty.

These Araucanians, among whom such expeditions are not unfrequent, are, according to the accounts of officers here, a very warlike people, well armed with bows, arrows, and lances: they make their onset in great hordes, with a wild yell, and with such fury and rapidity that it is not easy even for regular troops to resist. If this, however, can be firmly withstood, they are in a few minutes defeated and put to flight. When pursued, they escape shots and sabre strokes by the dexterity with which they fling themselves on either side of their horses; sometimes even hanging under the horse's belly while it is going at full gallop. When escape is impossible, they defend themselves to the last, preferring death to captivity.

From Rio Janeiro I had brought a letter of introduction to a once rich and still prosperous merchant in Conception, named Mendiburu; I immediately sought him out, and was received and entertained with the kindest hospitality. His house proved to be the same which, on my former visit to Conception, the then Governor had appointed for my accommodation. At that time many discontented spirits had already shown themselves, had assumed the appellation of patriots, and were persecuted by the Government; Mendiburu was one of these, and having made his escape, the Government, till its overthrow, had kept possession of his house.

My complaisant host, a little man, rather advanced in years, who in many respects was extremely useful to us, accompanied us, as soon as we had arranged our dress, to the President Freire. The latter received us in the full uniform of a general officer, with the most ceremonious politeness, but still kindly, although something of distrust might be perceived in his deportment.

Our circumstances with respect to Spain were known; and, as I afterwards learned, it was absurdly enough imagined, that Russia had designs upon Chili, and that these formed the secret motive of our visit. Freire, who had already distinguished himself as a general, is a stately-looking man, at that time about forty-five years of age, and of a very agreeable exterior; he was born in Talcaguana, of very poor parents, and, without enjoying any particular advantage of education, has raised himself, by his own merit alone, to the high rank he occupies.

After an unmeaning sort of conversation, consisting of little else than civilities, I endeavoured to procure the permission of the President for our naturalist and mineralogist to make a journey into the Cordilleras, which he, however, politely but positively refused, on the ground that the Chilians were at war with the people in the mountains. I afterwards learnt from

Mendiburu, that this was merely a pretence, as the President had already succeeded in establishing peace and an amicable league with the Araucanians. A small military escort would therefore have been amply sufficient to protect the travellers from all danger of annoyance; but here the weakness of the newly established government betrayed itself. They are distrustful of strangers, and act upon the old Spanish maxim,—to close the interior of the country against them. The recent discovery of gold and silver mines in the mountains, which was still kept secret, from the fear that foreign powers might covet these treasures, probably, also, contributed to a refusal which has undoubtedly proved, for the present, a serious loss to science. All the arguments I could urge to obviate the President's objections were ineffectual: all I could obtain for our learned associates was permission to travel round the bay of Conception and the environs of Talcaguana, for which a passport was made out; and a subaltern officer was appointed to accompany them, who in all probability had also his private instructions to see that the journey extended no farther.

Overwhelmed with courtesies and promises to make our residence here as agreeable as possible, we left the President, and concluded the day in pleasant society at the house of our host Mendiburu, who on the following morning accompanied us back to Talcaguana. He had the complaisance to surrender for our accommodation and the convenience of our astronomical observations, a large house belonging to him in Talcaguana, which had once been inhabited by La Pérouse. I took immediate possession of it, and our time was now very agreeably divided between the necessary attention to the repairs and provisioning of the ship, scientific observations, and the society of the hospitable natives.

The little town was soon filled with warlike tumult. A grenadier regiment from Conception marched in with drums beating and a very good band playing. The uniform was in the French fashion, clean and substantial; the muskets were in the best order.

Freire has most zealously exerted himself to raise a respectable army; but to bring a rabble of adventurers from all nations into proper discipline is no easy task, especially where there is not money enough to pay them punctually; even the officers are mostly foreigners, and, with few exceptions, ignorant and stupid beyond all belief. With such a soldiery, patriotism or enthusiasm in the cause is of course out of the question. The Chilian soldier fights like a robber, for the sake of the booty he hopes to acquire; and covetousness will form the foundation of his valour, till increase of population shall permit the organization of a national militia.

A few regiments had been sent over to the island of Quiquirino, perhaps in order to render desertion more difficult: here they had formed a camp, and were exercised in various manœuvres. The whole force, consisting of three thousand men, was destined, under the command of the President, to attack the island of Chiloe, the only spot still remaining in possession of the Spaniards. They were now waiting the arrival of the requisite vessels from Valparaiso.

On the 20th of January, amidst the thunder of the artillery, a new Constitution was proclaimed at Conception, signed there in great form by Freire, and afterwards read in many other towns of the Republic. Some of the inhabitants received it with enthusiasm, but it by no means gave satisfaction to all. In Talcaguana, opinions were much divided, and loudly and undisguisedly expressed. In every company the new Constitution became the chief subject of conversation, and often gave occasion to violent disputes. Even the ladies were not exempt from this political mania: they gave their opinions with unhesitating confidence and decision, and, in fact, often appeared fully as capable of forming a correct judgment as the men.

Without entering into these criticisms, I shall only remark, that one regulation of the Chilian Constitution must certainly be disadvantageous— the public exercise of any other religion than the Catholic is forbidden; Catholics only can fill civil offices (with the military such strictness is impracticable); nor is any one permitted to carry on a mechanical trade who does not belong to this Church.

If the advantage of universal toleration is so evident in the most flourishing states, how much more desirable must it be for one so thinly peopled, and where industry and knowledge are so little advanced.

We frequently received visits on board from the ladies and gentlemen of Chili; and once from an Araucanian chief, accompanied by his daughter and some attendants. A collation was prepared for the Araucanians, of which they heartily partook; and despising the knife and fork, helped themselves plentifully with their fingers. The meal being concluded, we made them some trifling presents, with which they were much delighted; the chief also begged a piastre, and his daughter (a true woman, though a savage,) a looking-glass. After she had contemplated her features for some time with much satisfaction, the treasure was passed from hand to hand among her people, who all appeared extremely well content with the reflection of their own faces, although, according to our ideas of beauty, none of them had any cause for vanity. They are of the middle stature, strongly built, and of dark complexions. Their hair is black, and hangs loosely over their shoulders; and their little Chinese eyes, and prominent cheek-bones, seemed to indicate an Asiatic origin. The expression of their faces is good-natured, lively, and rather intelligent. Their dress is very simple, consisting merely of a piece of many-coloured striped woollen stuff of their own manufacture: in shape, it is an oblong square, with a hole in the centre through which the head is passed, the longer ends hanging down to the knee before and behind, the shorter at each side falling over the shoulders, and the lower part of their limbs remaining bare. The Spanish Chilians call this garment a *pancho*, and often use it in winter as a surtout: among the common people it makes the daily, and sometimes even the only clothing.

The officers of the regiment stationed here politely gave a ball in our honour, which, as might be expected in this poor village, did not prove very brilliant; but as my young officers found plenty of pretty and agreeable partners, they were perfectly satisfied. The old custom of opening a ball with a minuet is still practised here, and the Chilians dance it remarkably well.

Besides the dances common among us, a sort of fandango is a favourite here: it is expressly adapted to display the graces of a fine figure to the best advantage, and is danced by two persons, whose picturesque attitudes and motions are accompanied on the guitar, and by tender songs, according in expression with the pantomimical representations of the dance.

We determined to return the complaisance of the natives by giving a ball on board our ship to our acquaintances in Talcaguana, and some from Conception. My officers made every effort to surpass the Chilians in the elegance of their entertainment; and having been detained on shore during their preparations, and till the hour appointed for the ball, I was really astonished to see how much they had been able to achieve. The deck was changed into a large illuminated saloon, decorated with fine myrtle trees, luxuriant garlands, and bouquets of flowers of every colour, exhaling the sweetest perfumes, and appropriate transparencies in the background opposite the entrance. The cabins had been cleared for refreshment-rooms; and the musicians, concealed behind a curtain, were to pour forth their animating strains unseen by the dancers. The cheerful scene was rapidly filled with cheerful faces; graceful figures moved in the lively dances; and love and beauty alone seemed to preside within the joyous precincts. But suddenly a universal confusion and panic terror was spread among the company, and chiefly among the ladies. Some suspicious simpleton or mischievous wag had whispered that we had a design of secretly weighing anchor during this festivity, and sailing away with our beautiful prisoners. My friend Mendiburu, however, at length succeeded in banishing this ridiculous apprehension, and restoring tranquillity. Pleasure and confidence again reigned over the revels, till the sun stood high in the heavens; and like every other earthly enjoyment, even our ball drew to a close, though it bade fair to linger long in the recollection as well of our returning guests as of some of the young entertainers.

The delightful weather tempted us, soon after this, to make an excursion to the opposite shores of the bay, and visit the ruins of the old town of Conception. Mendiburu was of the party, as were all of our scientific brethren, and as many of the officers as duty permitted to be absent. Very early, on a beautiful morning, we distributed our party in three large boats, and rowed, in two hours, to the destined point. We landed at the village of Pencu, which, like Portici upon Herculaneum, is built upon the ruins of the former town of Conception, and whose inhabitants live quietly and cheerfully over the graves of their unfortunate predecessors, and disturb themselves little with the thought, that the same fate may bury them one day in a living tomb.

About fifteen houses, surrounded by gardens, lie scattered here over a lovely plain, watered by the small river St. Peter. Nature here appears more luxuriant and productive than at Talcaguana. The mountains which encircle this valley rise gently to a moderate height, and delight the eye by the freshness of the shrubs with which they are covered.

While we gave chase to many kinds of birds and insects for the improvement of our collection, the sailors threw out a great net, and took a quantity of shell and other fish with which the sea abounds in this neighbourhood, and which make the chief subsistence of the poorer classes of people. The environs of this village are considered the loveliest district round the bay, and infinitely surpassing Talcaguana in the beauty of its scenery. Few remains of the old town are visible. The earth seems to have actually opened and swallowed it up, leaving scarcely a trace behind. Even the yawning gulph in which it sunk has filled again, so that it is only here and there upon the plain that some fragment of a former dwelling reminds one of the fearful catastrophe.

The inhabitants of Talcaguana and Conception make excursions to Pencu, to examine, as a curiosity, a water-mill established there by some foreigner. We found it so out of repair as to be unserviceable, and the owner complained that he could find no one capable of mending it. The wheat is here ground to flour by beating it in stone pots with heavy wooden clubs; which may serve to give some idea of the progress the Chilians have made in the useful arts.

Mendiburu possessed an estate near Pencu, where we partook of a pleasant meal under the shade of fruit-trees. After dinner the whole company went shooting, and in the course of a few hours had killed several hundred water-birds of various kinds. The flocks in which they fly are sometimes so numerous as to darken the air. During our absence such a one was descried from the ship; it appeared a solid mass of about ten fathoms broad, and its flight lasted full three hours.

The repairs of our ship had gone on quickly, and the time approached for our leaving Chili, when we perceived that the friendliness and civility we had hitherto experienced from the inhabitants was changing into reserve and evident distrust. Secret cabals were going on against us; and even the Government seemed inclined to act, if not with positive hostility, at least violently and arbitrarily towards us.

The attention of the unreflecting and easily excited Chilians had first been attracted by the mustachios worn by one of my companions. They took him for a disguised Spaniard, who had accompanied us to sow discontents, and gain back the hearts of the people to the old government. Other misrepresentations may also have been made against us; but we were neither able to discover them, nor the actual intentions entertained towards us.

When the ship was ready to sail, and I thought to quit Talcaguana in a few days, I returned to Conception to take leave of the President Freire. While on the road, being mounted on a spirited horse, I had got a little the start of my companions, and was stopping on a height to contemplate the beautiful landscape around me, when a well-dressed young man, coming from the direction of the town, suddenly met me, stood still, looking attentively at me for some moments, and then asked if I were the Captain of the Russian frigate. On my answering in the affirmative, after ascertaining that we were not observed, he said, "You are aware that the two parties in this country are differently disposed towards you. The day after to-morrow the officers of the regiment in Talcaguana will give you a farewell ball, when they intend to overpower the Russian officers, and take them prisoners. I have adopted this method of making you acquainted with the design; be on your guard." With these words he disappeared among the high shrubs. As soon as my companions came up, I took Mendiburu aside, and told him what I had just heard. Honourable and warm-hearted, my friend at first grew pale with astonishment and vexation; but, after a few moments' consideration, he felt convinced, and assured me, that the thing was impossible, and that my unknown monitor must be in error. At the same time we both determined, immediately on our arrival in Conception, to mention the circumstance to the President. Freire received me in a very friendly manner, and so confidently affirmed the project attributed to his officers, to be a mere "coinage of the brain" of my informant, that I trusted to his opinion, and thought no more of it, especially as our own ball had furnished a proof how easily the silliest and most groundless reports could gain credit.

After leaving the President, I passed the remainder of the day, and slept, at the house of my friend Mendiburu. As I was preparing to go to bed, I heard a gentle knock at my room door; I opened it, and a servant of the house came timidly in. He told me that he was a Spaniard, and had been a sailor on board a frigate captured by the Chilians, and that his present master had taken him into his service, when a prisoner of war. He then gave me, under the most earnest injunctions not to betray him, the same caution which I had before received, adding some curses on the Chilian Government and people, whom he declared to be altogether a set of vagabonds and thieves. This repeated warning was too striking not to excite some apprehension. I took all the circumstances into consideration; and though the motive for such a proceeding remained perfectly incomprehensible, I still resolved to take measures for my security, in case it should be really attempted. I passed a sleepless night, and early in the morning bade adieu to my kind host, to whom I was unable to impart my new cause of anxiety, and hastened back to Talcaguana. On my arrival there, I found cards inviting myself and all my officers to a ball on the following evening: so far, therefore, the information I had received was correct. To avoid the appearance of suspicion, I accepted the invitation, and went to the ball accompanied by a few of my officers. The rest remained on board the ship, having placed her so as to bring her guns to bear upon the house in which the ball was given, and to command the respect of the neighbourhood. Thus Talcaguana was at our mercy; nor had we any thing to fear, either from the armed corvette, or the battery on shore; the former being so situated that it must needs have struck to our first broadside, and the latter mounting only six guns quite unfit for use, and resting upon broken carriages. We had also removed our observatory, and conveyed all our effects on board. These imposing preparations did not in all probability remain unobserved; at all events, the ball passed off quietly enough; but it was remarkable that very few of the officers who had given it were present; and instead of the gaiety which had reigned on the two former occasions, the greatest constraint was evident in the deportment of the company, who separated at an unusually early hour.

At daybreak we weighed anchor, to resume our voyage; but before we were in motion, my faithful friend Mendiburu, who had travelled in the night from Conception, came on board with the news that a Chilian frigate and a corvette, which had arrived two days before from Valparaiso with troops, now lay at anchor at the mouth of the bay, and had received orders to prevent our departure. He had no idea what could have induced his government, against which he was excessively indignant, to meditate such an outrage; but he felt assured that the ships were by no means in a condition to obey. When in full sail, I parted from Mendiburu, for the second time, with hearty thanks for his sympathy and assistance.

I now ordered the ship and guns to be prepared for battle, in case it should prove necessary to force our way out. We proceeded with a fresh and favouring breeze so rapidly, that in an hour's time we could distinguish the two vessels lying at anchor near the island of Quiquirino. As we approached, a gun was fired from the frigate, on which signal both ships got under sail, and took a direction that would enable them to oppose our progress. No longer doubting their hostile intentions, I lessened my sail to make the ship more manageable during the expected engagement. The matches were lighted, and every one stood at his post; but the Chilian frigate, a bad sailer, having run too far to leeward, could not come up to the assistance of the corvette which endeavoured to dispute our passage; but clearly perceiving, when within gun-shot, that we were prepared to resist an attack, found it most prudent to sail peaceably on, contenting herself with calling something to us through a trumpet, which we could not understand. Pursuing our course in an opposite direction, we were soon at a considerable distance from the corvette, and then saw the frigate tacking to follow us; but having already greatly the advantage, and the mouth of the bay clear before us, we rehoisted our sails, and without waiting for further evidence of Chilian hostility, stood out to sea; thus escaping attempts upon our liberty, the real motive of which, perhaps, was a desire to employ our ships in the transport of troops to Chiloe. The two English whalers had already been taken possession of for this purpose, without the consent of their captains.

The result of our observations on land are as follows:

Latitude from Mendiburu's house in Talcaguana	36° 42' 15"
West Longitude	73° 8' 20"
Declination of the needle	14° East
Inclination	80° 4'

The tide is here quite imperceptible. During the whole time of our stay, Reaumur's thermometer stood between 15 and 17 degrees.

THE DANGEROUS
ARCHIPELAGO.

THE many islands composing this Archipelago, and which the little coralline insects have built in the midst of the ocean, are so low, that they are invisible at a very trifling distance. From this cause they have often, in darkness or bad weather, proved dangerous to navigation, and have thence derived their name. It was my intention now, to ascertain exactly the geographical position of the islands which I had discovered on my former voyage. O Tahaiti was to serve as a point from which to determine the longitude, and at the same time to furnish us with provisions.

I directed my course to this Archipelago, between the parallels of 15 and 16 degrees of South latitude, because this is not the usual track of merchants' ships, nor has it been taken in voyages of discovery, so that I thought it not improbable that we might fall in with other unknown islands. In pursuance of this plan, we steered north-west, for the above mentioned parallel. An uninterrupted fresh south wind having carried us six hundred and sixty miles forwards in three days, brought us into the hot climate so suddenly, that we were much inconvenienced by it. The island of Juan Fernandez, whither the Spaniards, when masters in Chili, used to banish criminals and republicans, lay on our left, and the little uninhabited rocky islands of Felix and Ambrosia at a little distance on our right. After rapidly gaining the Southern Tropic, our voyage, though pleasant, was far more tranquil; the slightness of the motion between the Tropics, admits of employment on board a ship, for which a sailor has generally little opportunity; even drawings may be executed in the neatest manner.

On the 17th February we found ourselves under eighteen degrees of South latitude, and a hundred and five degrees longitude. The weather continued fine and serene, and our men expressed a wish to interrupt the uniformity of their lives, by getting up a play. The theatre was prepared, the play-bills given out, and the orchestra had even made the signal for the company to assemble, when our merriment was suddenly changed into terror and distress; another sailor fell overboard. He had been keeping watch on the fore-mast, to provide for our safety against land and shallows, in this untried region, and having neglected to secure his own, fell a sacrifice to his thoughtlessness. Being injured by the fall, he immediately sunk, and all our efforts to save him proved fruitless. Separated as we had long been from our native country, the loss of a member of our little society, thus bound together through good or ill fortune, was sensibly felt; the poor fellow was, besides, one of our best sailors: in the most violent storms, he had often executed the most dangerous tasks at the mast-head with the greatest skill, and now in the finest weather, with the ship moving in a manner scarcely perceptible, was he destined to end, thus suddenly, his active and useful life.

Having sailed four thousand miles in three weeks, since we left Chili, we reached the neighbourhood of the dangerous Archipelago. By degrees we now lost, contrary to all rule in this climate, the south-east trade-wind, which had hitherto been so favourable to us, and contrary winds from the West and North brought us very bad weather. An opinion has been hitherto entertained, that the coral islands, from lying so low and in small masses, could produce no change in the atmosphere, and that the trade-winds, to which they offered no obstruction, would continue to blow uninterruptedly in their neighbourhood. Repeated experience has, however, convinced me that this is an error, and that these little islands, at certain seasons, often cause variations from the ordinary tropical weather.

On the 26th of February, we entered 16° of latitude, and 129° of longitude. The wind blew from the West: black clouds labouring upwards, covered the sky; violent and sudden gusts expended their fury on us, and lightnings flashed from every corner of the horizon. The night was really dreadful, and the tempest continued to rage, through a darkness which, but for the lightning, would have been total, while torrents of rain swept our decks. Nor did the return of light bring us much relief; when about noon the heavens cleared for a short time, and allowed us a little respite; the storm set in again with renewed violence, and for four days and nights we were condemned to struggle with this tremendous weather. It is surprising how such tempests can arise at so great a distance from land. In the ship Rurik, in this same region, at the same season of year, I have before met with similar though scarcely such furious storms. On the 2nd of March the tropical wind returned, and brought with it clearer weather. It was indeed very hot, (Reaumur's thermometer did not fall even in the night below 24,) but the whole crew continued in good health. On this evening we calculated that we were in 15° 15' latitude, and 139° 40' longitude; and just as the sun was sinking, the man at the mast-head called out that land was in sight. The pleasure of making a new discovery set all our telescopes in motion, and before night set in we plainly distinguished a very low, thickly wooded island. Since no navigator, to my knowledge, had ever been here before, and the newest charts described nothing but empty space, we conceived we had a right to consider ourselves the first discoverers, and named the island, after our ship, Predpriatie: we now tacked to stand out to sea for the night, and at break of day again made towards the island, under feelings of strong excitement. The many telescopes which our eager curiosity pointed towards its object, seemed each endued with the magical power of conveying different images to the sight. Some of us saw what others saw not, till these delusions of the imagination vanished before the conviction produced by rising columns of smoke visible to all, that the island was inhabited. We could soon afterwards, from the mast-head, perceive its entire extent. The dazzling whiteness of the coral shore fringed a bright green ground upon which rose a forest of palms; and we distinguished canoes moving upon a large lake in the centre of the island. By rapid degrees, we approached so near that every object became perceptible with the naked eye. A tall, strong, dark-coloured race of naked savages were assembling on the shore, gazing on the ship in great agitation, with gestures of astonishment. Some were arming with long spears and clubs, others kindling piles of wood, probably, that the smoke might be a signal to neighbouring islands of their requiring assistance against the unknown sea-monster. From pretty huts of plaited reeds, under the shade of bread-fruit trees, the women, some of them with children in their arms, were flying to conceal themselves in the forest. Such was the commotion our appearance occasioned in this little community. A few heroes summoned courage enough to advance, with threatening attitudes, to the margin of the shore; but no single canoe, though many lay on the coast, ventured to approach us. Judging from their size and the good arrangement of their sails, these canoes seem intended for visits to other and even distant islands. We sailed quite round our new discovery without finding any haven by which we could effect a landing; and the sea being tempestuous, with a high and boisterous surf, we were compelled to renounce our desire of becoming more intimately acquainted with the Predpriatians. The unclouded sky enabled us, nevertheless, to determine by observation the exact latitude and longitude of this little island, whose greatest extent is only four miles from E.N.E. to W.S.W. The latitude of its central point is 15° 58' 18" South, and its longitude, 140° 11' 30". The variation of the needle was 4° East.

When we had finished our observations, I steered a westerly course for the island of Araktschief, discovered in the year 1819 by the Russian Captain Bellingshausen, in order to convince myself that it was actually not the one we had just quitted.

At four o'clock in the afternoon we could already see this island from the mast-head, and we reached it before sunset. It bears, with respect to size and circumstances, so close a resemblance to that of Predpriatie, that they might easily be mistaken, if their relative situations were not exactly known.

From our observation, we found the latitude of the centre of the island of Araktschief 15° 51' 20" South; and the longitude 140° 50' 50". According to Captain Bellingshausen's chart, the latitude is 15° 51', the longitude 140°

52'. Unable to discover any traces of inhabitants on this island, we should have supposed there were none, had not Captain Bellingshausen ascertained the contrary.

At night we retired to some distance from the island and lay-to, that we might not, in the darkness, strike on any unknown land. At break of day I steered a north-west course, to see the island of Romanzow, (which I had formerly discovered when with the ship Rurik,) and convince myself of the accuracy of the astronomical observations then made. At eight o'clock in the morning we could see the north point of the group of Wolchonsky Islands, recently discovered by Captain Bellingshausen. When they lay seven miles off us, to the South, we found the longitude, according to our chronometers, 142° 2' 38". Bellingshausen considered it to be 142° 7' 42".

From failure of wind, we could not make the island of Romanzow till the morning of the 8th of March. We then took advantage of the clearness of the heavens to ascertain, by the distance between the sun and moon, its exact longitude, which is 144° 28'. According to the observations we had made in the ship Rurik, it was 144° 24', consequently there was a difference of only four minutes.

We now steered due West, in order to learn whether the island which, on my voyage in the Rurik, I had named after Admiral Spiridow, was really a new discovery, or, as has been said, only the most southerly of the King George's Islands. A fresh wind favoured our course, and at six o'clock in the afternoon we could see this island, my discovery of which has been denied, lying before us at a distance of six miles westward.

At the same time, we could distinguish from the mast-head the southern part of another island, lying due North, with open water between the two. We were in 14° 41' 36" South latitude, and 144° 55' longitude. During the night we were becalmed, but in the morning a fresh breeze sprang up directly in our teeth, and the current carried us so far to the South, that, even from the mast, we could no longer see land. Under these circumstances, to attempt to regain the Spiridow Island would have been attended by too great loss of time; so that we remained uncertain whether this and the other, which we saw in the North, were the two King George's Islands or not. I can only say, that if they really are so, their discoverer has given their geographical position very inaccurately.

The south-east trade-wind had ceased to befriend us, and shifting gusts from the north-west and south blew with such violence as frequently to tear our sails, accompanied by incessant rain and storm. The sea being at the same time remarkably calm, proved that we were surrounded by islands, and that, in consequence, the greatest caution was required in sailing, especially as the currents in this region are often very strong. We soon saw land directly before us; and as in the neighbourhood of all coral islands the depth of the sea cannot be sounded at a distance of fifty fathoms from the shore, we approached within a mile of it. This island stretches ten miles in length, from East to West, and is only four miles broad; it appeared to be a narrow strip of land, thickly overgrown with low bushes, surrounding a lake in the centre. Sea-birds only, of which we saw a vast number, appeared to inhabit this waste. The latitude of the middle of this island we found to be 15° 27', and its longitude 145° 31' 12". According to the chart of Admiral Krusenstern, it may be the island called Carlshof, discovered in the year 1722, by Roggewin, the geographical position of which is given differently on almost every chart, and whose very existence has been disputed. We were now in the midst of the dangerous Archipelago, and consulted our safety by riding every night only in parts which we had surveyed during the day.

After reiterated nightly storms and rains, we shaped our course, with full sails, on the return of fine weather, due East, for the Palliser Islands discovered by Captain Cook, and reached them in a few hours. On board the Rurik, I had only seen their northern side, and I now wished, astronomically, to determine the southern. Cook mentions these islands very superficially, so that navigators have fallen into many errors concerning them. The group consists of a number of small islands connected by coral reefs, which form a circular chain, and enclose a large piece of water. When we had reached the southern point of the east Pallisers, we saw a ridge stretching ten miles westward to two small islands, and thence taking a northern direction to unite itself at a considerable distance with larger ones.

Cook, from his own account, did not approach near enough to see this ridge, and from a distance mistook the two little woody islands it embraces for the most southerly of a distinct cluster, which he calls the fourth group of Palliser Islands. I can maintain that there are only three such groups, as the map which accompanies this volume will show. At noon we found our latitude to be 15° 42' 19", and the longitude 146° 21' 6".

The above-mentioned two small islands on the reef lay directly North, and the southern part of the first cluster of Pallisers was no longer visible. Viewed from this spot, the smaller ones might have been mistaken by us also for part of another group, if we had not previously ascertained that they were connected with the first by means of the reef. The second and third group could also be seen from this point; the former to the S.E. the latter S.W.

At six o'clock in the evening, we found ourselves near the eastern point of the third group, and saw from the mast-head the Greigh Islands, discovered by Captain Bellingshausen. We now steered between these two groups, in order to free ourselves from the Archipelago, and regain the open sea. Again the night was tempestuous; but a calm occurred in the course of it, which, had it lasted longer, would have been dangerous, as a strong current was carrying us towards the shore. The morning sun, as usual in the Torrid Zone, dispersed the clouds and restored the beautiful blue of the tropical sky. We soon lost sight of land, but a black cloud still lowered in that part of the horizon where it had disappeared; a proof how powerfully these masses of coral attract thunder clouds. We now recovered the south-east wind, and favoured by it, took the shortest way to O Tahaiti. All the longitudes in the dangerous Archipelago which I have given, (without entering into the manner in which they were calculated,) are made out by means of the chronometer. This, on arriving at O Tahaiti, was found six minutes fifty seconds wrong; and the longitudes here given have been rectified accordingly.

The following is from our observations the situation of the Palliser Islands:—

South point of the first group	Lat. 15° 34' 25"
	Long. 146° 6' 49"
The two small islands to the West of the first group	Lat. 15° 30' 15"
	Long. 146° 20' 50"
The Eastern point of the third group	Lat. 15° 44' 52"
	Long. 146° 28' 2".

Most of the islands of this Archipelago are inhabited, but hitherto little is known of the natives, who are shy, and endeavour to avoid any intercourse with navigators. Byron landed by force on one of these islands; in the struggle many of the inhabitants were killed, the rest put to flight, and the provision of cocoa-nuts found in their huts plundered. Tradition may perhaps have exaggerated this attack. Cook also permitted some of his crew to land, who indeed met with no resistance, but their presents were received with the greatest indifference, and stones were thrown after them on their departure. Captain Bellingshausen, in the year 1820, wished to land on one of these islands, but the natives opposed his intention so seriously that he relinquished it rather than use force. These people resemble the O Tahaitians, their neighbours and relatives, in appearance and language; and when the latter are farther advanced in civilization, it may be presumed that intercourse with them will effect a considerable amelioration in the condition of the other South Sea islanders.

O TAHAITI.

THIS beautiful island, so richly endowed by nature with every thing that its simple and innocent natives can require for the enjoyment of existence, was perhaps first seen by the Spanish voyager Quiras, when, in the year 1606, he made an expedition from Lima, "to win," as a countryman of his expresses it, "souls for Heaven, and kingdoms for Spain." Since, however, the position pointed out by him is extremely incorrect, it is uncertain whether the island which he called Sagittaria was really O Tahaiti or not. More probably, the honour of the discovery belongs to the English Captain Wallis, who in the year 1767 landed there, and took possession of the country by a solemn declaration, in the name of his King. As, however, the Tahaitians did not understand him, this act remained unknown to them; and, notwithstanding a subsequent renewal, has fallen into oblivion. Captain Wallis gave it the name of King George the Third's Island.

Eight months after him, the French Captain Bougainville visited it; and not knowing that Captain Wallis had been there before him, considered himself the first discoverer, and called it, from the most remarkable custom of the natives, *Nouvelle Cythère*, but heard that they themselves called it Tahaiti, or with the article, O Tahaiti; and this name it has retained.

The celebrated Englishman, Cook, stopped there in each of his three voyages, between the years 1769 and 1778. He remained much longer in communication with the inhabitants than any of his predecessors had done; brought back Omai, to whom in London it had been attempted to give an European education, to his native land, and made use of the narrations he obtained from him during the voyage. Since that time, Cook and his companions, particularly the two Forsters, father and son, have given us considerable information concerning the condition of the Tahaitians before their conversion to the Christian faith.

To estimate the effect of this great change, we must compare Christian Tahaiti as it now is, with the accounts these early voyagers have left us of its heathen times; and as every reader may not be conveniently able to do so, a short review of them may not be considered unwelcome.

The Society Islands, of which Tahaiti is the largest, are, like many others, either fragments of a Southern continent swallowed up by earthquake, or a mass of rock ejected from the bottom of the sea by subterranean fire, which gradually becoming covered with a fertile soil, is now adorned by the most beautiful vegetation. It consists of two peninsulas united by a narrow isthmus, which together are about one hundred and twenty miles in circumference; towards the centre of each rise wild rocky mountains, intersected by deep ravines, from the side of which, thickly wooded almost to their summits, flow numerous streamlets of pure transparent water, forming the most picturesque cascades as they descend from every direction into the sea. The high mountains are uninhabited, and the settlements made only in the valleys, more especially in the low land between the mountains and the sea-shore.

In these charming amphitheatrical landscapes, their houses, consisting only of roofs resting on stakes, surrounded and shaded by bananas, bread-fruit and cocoa-trees, are scattered at small distances from each other.

Attached to every house are enclosed fields, where the proprietors cultivate their yams, sweet potatoes, and other wholesome and pleasant roots, which form their chief nourishment.

The rest of the cultivated land is filled by plantations of bananas and plantains, or little forests of cocoa and bread-fruit trees, so luxuriantly interwoven, that the burning rays of the sun cannot penetrate to injure the bright verdure which clothes the soil. The neatly kept grass footpaths leading through these groves from one dwelling to another, are variegated with flowers of the richest colours and most fragrant perfumes, and enlivened by the notes of innumerable birds arrayed in all the splendid hues of the Tropics. Although Tahaiti is only seventeen degrees from the Equator, the heat is so much moderated by refreshing breezes that it is very supportable even to an European. Bougainville never found it above twenty-two, and often under eighteen degrees of Reaumur. That indeed was during the winter; but even in January, the middle of the Tahaitian summer, the atmosphere is much cooled by the frequent rains. The air is usually dry, clear, and particularly healthy; sick people brought ashore from a sea voyage recover rapidly. Here are neither ants, musquitoes, nor any of the tormenting insects so common in tropical climates; no beast of prey, no destructive worm nor serpent; even the scorpion (of which a small sort is to be met with) here loses its poison. The only plague of this kind is a large rat, which does much mischief in the fields, and sometimes even bites the Tahaitians during their sleep.

Bougainville says, "The inhabitants of Tahaiti consist of two distinct races, which remain such, although their language and manners are the same, and they appear to mingle indiscriminately with each other. One, the most numerous, produces the tallest men, commonly six feet and upwards; and I have never seen better proportioned, or finer forms. A sculptor could not choose a more suitable model for a Mars or a Hercules. There is nothing to distinguish their features from those of Europeans; and if they were clothed, and less exposed to the air and the burning sun, they would be quite as fair. Their hair is usually black (Wallis saw fair people, and

Banks even Albinos). The other race is of middle stature, with coarse curling hair, and resembles the Mulatto in complexion and features."

Cook and his companions considered this difference among the Tahaitians to arise from the circumstance of the tall fair race, (called Eris, which is pronounced *Yeri*,) the more distinguished class, being less exposed to the sun and to hard labour, and their women more reserved and less licentious.

We were however more inclined to agree with Bougainville, who supposed the dark Tahaitians to be the original inhabitants, and the Yeris invaders, who at some remote period had subjugated them; for the latter are the exclusive possessors of the land; the others obtaining only a certain remuneration in fruits and vegetables for cultivating the fields and plantations of their masters. The kings and all great personages are of this race, which is held by the common people in much veneration.

That the language and customs of both races should have assimilated is natural; but with respect to their intermarriages, Bougainville was in error; the pride of the Yeris keeps them aloof from any such connections, which, had they subsisted, must have long since destroyed the broad and acknowledged line of distinction. It is, however, only fair to confess, that this hypothesis of an invasion is unsupported by any Tahaitian tradition.

"The men of both races," continues this traveller, "allow the lower part of the beard to grow, but shave the whiskers and the upper lip. Some cut their hair short off, others bind it together at the top of the head; both hair and beard they grease with the oil of the cocoa-nut. A girdle round the middle often serves for their only clothing; but the people of rank generally wear a large piece of stuff which falls as low as the knee. This is the principal garment of the women, who put it on in a very becoming manner. The female Yeris, who never expose themselves to the sun, and wear a hat of reeds adorned with flowers, which shades the face, are fairer than the men: their features are handsome, but they are chiefly remarkable for the beauty of their figures, which are not spoiled by the artifices of European fashions. They paint their cheeks red, and colour the lower part of the body dark blue, as an ornament and a distinction of rank.

"Both sexes are tattooed, and both hang rows of pearls or flowers through holes pierced in their ears. The greatest cleanliness reigns among them; they bathe regularly, and wash themselves before and after meals."

The descriptions of other travellers agree perfectly with this; all appear to feel the greatest kindness for these "nurselings of joyous nature," as some one calls them; and to have been particularly charmed with the women, of whom Wallis says, "They are all handsome, and some excessively lovely."

The companions of Cook also speak in the highest terms of their attractions. Their tall and slender figures; the form of their faces, which is agreeable, though rather round than oval; the tender transparency of their skin; the complexions which, whether fair or brown, are always blooming; the expressive eyes, now flashing fire and now swimming in tenderness; the small white, even teeth, and fascinating smile, are rapturously described by the younger Forster.

The nose only is defective in these beauties, it is usually too flat, but may sometimes be seen as perfectly formed as in the females of Europe.

The curse, "in the sweat of thy brow shalt thou eat bread," falls harmless on the Tahaitians. Three bread-fruit trees are sufficient for a man's subsistence during a year; and he has here only to stretch out his hand to obtain this and many other fruits whose variety may please his palate. Nutritious roots are cultivated with great ease; and the sea yields abundance of shell and other fish, for the trifling trouble of catching it: the brooks also contain fish, and a species of crab. The opulent eat fowls and pigs roasted over hot stones in a hole in the ground, the flavour of which is very agreeable even to an European; and, by way of variety, they roast *dogs* which have been fed upon vegetables, and are considered great delicacies.

Several families often live together in the same house, in the greatest concord. Their furniture consists simply of a few ingeniously-woven mats for sleeping on, and some vessels made of gourds and cocoa-nut shells.

The disposition of the Tahaitians is gentle, benevolent, open, gay, and peaceable, although some of them show scars of wounds received in war, which prove that they are not deficient in courage. To hatred and revenge they are wholly strangers. Hardly and unjustly as Cook sometimes treated them, he was pardoned immediately that he required their assistance, and showed the slightest wish to pacify them. Individuals of his crew often ventured to pass the nights alone and unarmed upon the island: they were every where received with the greatest hospitality, and overwhelmed with marks of friendship. The simple inhabitants, wholly devoid of envy, rejoiced in each other's good fortune, and when one received a present, all seemed equally gratified. Their feelings readily broke out either into smiles or tears: even men were often seen to weep; and their joys and sorrows were as fugitive as those of children. Nor are their minds more stable: notwithstanding the great curiosity with which they gazed at and required an explanation of every object in the ship, it was as impossible, says the elder Forster, to rivet their attention for any time, as to make quicksilver stand still.

They seemed incapable of either mental or bodily effort, and their time was passed in indolence and enjoyment. They were, however, skilful in manufacturing a soft paper from the barks of trees; nets and lines from the fibres of the cocoa-nut; and hooks from muscle-shells; in weaving their rush mats, and especially in building canoes and war-boats. The latter, large enough to contain forty men and upwards, were made of planks laboriously split from the trunks of trees with sharp stones, for want of better implements, fastened together with cocoa threads, and well caulked. The value they set on our axes and nails may therefore be easily imagined.

Like all islanders, they are expert seamen, but especially dexterous in swimming and diving. They fetch any thing with ease from the bottom of the sea, even at very considerable depths. The upsetting of a boat causes them no uneasiness; men and women swim round it till they succeed in righting it again; and then, baling out the water, continue their voyage with the utmost unconcern.

These voyages, sometimes extending to considerable distances, have made the observation of the stars, their only guides, absolutely necessary to them. They have thus attained some astronomical knowledge.

They distinguish the planets from the fixed stars, and call the former by particular names. They divide the year into thirteen months of twenty-nine days each, with the exception of one, which has less, apparently for the purpose of reconciling this lunar with a solar year. The day and night are each divided into six parts of two hours each, which they measure exactly in the day by the position of the sun, and at night by the stars. Medical men have considered them to possess much skill in surgery, from the kindly healing of wounds which, by their scars, have evidently been severe.

The Tahaitians are particularly distinguished by their superior civilization from all other savages, among whom indeed they scarcely deserve to be ranked. Their language sounds agreeably, and is not difficult to learn. The vowels occur much more frequently than the consonants, our c, g, k, s, and p, being entirely wanting. Cook and his companions made considerable progress in it; and one of them says—"It is rich in figurative modes of expression; and I am convinced that a nearer acquaintance with it would place it on a level with the most distinguished for boldness and power of imagery."

By means of this knowledge of their language, however imperfect, many details concerning the religion of the Tahaitians were gained. The elder Forster enters rather at large into the subject.

They believed in one supreme God, *Athua-rahai*, creator and governor of the world, and of all other gods. They gave him a consort, who however was not of the same nature, but of a material and very firm substance, and therefore called *O-te-Papa*, that is to say, *Rock*. From this pair proceeded a goddess of the moon, the gods of the stars, the winds, and the sea, and the protecting deities of the several islands. After the chief god had created the sun, he conveyed his consort, the mighty Rock, from the West to the East over the sea: in their progress, some portions of her substance separated from her, and formed the islands.

Besides the gods of the second rank, they believed also in inferior deities, and in a wicked genius, who killed men suddenly at the requisition of the priests—an article of faith which this order doubtless found very convenient. They also supposed that a genius dwelt in every man, thinking and feeling in him, and separated himself from the body after death, but without removing from it; often inhabiting the wooden images which are erected in the burial-places, but sometimes stealing at night into their habitations, and killing the sleepers, whose hearts and entrails he devoured. This belief in ghosts is perhaps not more universal in Tahaiti than among civilized nations.

According to another of Cook's companions, the supreme God united departed souls with his own existence, which was signified by the phrase, "He eats them." This was purification, after which the soul, or the genius, reached the abode of eternal happiness. If a man, for some months before his death, had kept himself apart from women, he did not require this purification, but went direct to Heaven. The pride of the Yeris prompted them to believe in a Heaven peculiar to themselves, where they should associate only with their equals in birth.

The Tahaitians of rank had each a *Marai* sacred to themselves, and which served for their religious assemblies. The greatest and most solemn of these meetings were held at the Marai of the Kings. Here the priests harangued the people; and here was performed the rite which stained the otherwise amiable character of these islanders—the offering of human sacrifices! Cook was once present at one of these detestable oblations, and describes it circumstantially. Its object was to propitiate the assistance of the Gods, in a war about to be undertaken.

The victim was always of the lower class. He was first killed, and the ceremonies were afterwards performed by the priests, and many prayers recited, in presence of the King and people. One of the formalities was the presentation of the left eye to the King, which however he did not receive. From this, Cook infers that the Tahaitians had at some period been eaters of human flesh, and that this morsel was offered to the King as a delicacy. If this conjecture be well-founded, which I think it is not, so horrible an appetite must have long since disappeared, as not a trace of it now remains. It is besides altogether contrary to the character and manners of the people. So, indeed, is the oblation of human victims; but this horrible rite had certainly been introduced by the priests, for the purpose of attracting towards their office an increased degree of veneration and awe. The burial of the dead was accompanied by many religious ceremonies, but with the birth of a child, or the celebration of marriage, their religion was no way concerned.

If a woman bore her lover a child, which he acknowledged to be his, the marriage was concluded without further ceremony, but was easily dissolved and a new connexion formed.

A married man would sometimes entertain a concubine, but never had more than one wife. The kings only formed an exception to this rule. The last monarch married at the same time the four daughters of a neighbouring king, and during our visit they were all living and respected as his widows. One only of them had brought him children; and when during the latter years of his government he became a convert to the Christian religion, this one only passed for his lawful consort.

In both peninsulas of Tahaiti the form of government was monarchical, and each had its own king, assisted by a council of Yeris, whom he consulted on all important occasions. These were held in great veneration among the people. No one, not even a female or a Yeri of the highest rank, might appear before them without uncovering the upper part of the body—a token of respect which was usually paid only to the Gods in prayer or in passing a Marai. Before the princesses, the female sex only uncovered themselves. All his subjects were much attached to the sovereign, who reigned under a most singular law of succession.

As soon as a son was born to him, the sovereignty passed from the king to the infant, in whose name, and during whose minority only, the father continued to exercise the Regency.

The several districts were governed by deputies chosen from the class of Yeris, who were also the sole administrators of justice; which amongst this well-disposed people was generally very mild. The punishments in a great measure depend on the injured party, and consist chiefly in stripes. A native assured me that thieves are sometimes hung on a tree; but they more frequently escape with a few strokes, or sometimes altogether with impunity.

The two kingdoms of Tahaiti were often in a state of mutual warfare, though they sometimes fought as allies against a common enemy. Cook and his companions saw the preparations for a war with the neighbouring island of Eimeo, and were present at a review of his naval force by the King O Tu. From the number of warriors who manned this fleet, the elder Forster estimated the entire population at not less than a hundred and thirty thousand souls. According to his opinion, Tahaiti was capable of containing and supporting an infinitely greater number of inhabitants, and he therefore conjectured that in a short time it would be found greatly increased. Experience has unfortunately proved this inference to be erroneous, as will appear in the sequel.

Notwithstanding their usually gentle character, they treated their prisoners of war with barbarity, but in their defence may be urged the well-known fact, that in the heat of battle an unwonted rage will sometimes take possession of the best disposed minds, even amongst civilized nations; and it was only while this unnatural excitement lasted that the conduct of the Tahaitians laid them open to the imputation of cruelty.

Both sexes and all ranks were given to stealing; and so dexterous were they in plundering the Europeans, that notwithstanding the utmost vigilance and precaution, few days passed without something being stolen. The young, beautiful, and noble Marorai stole, as the younger Forster relates, a pair of sheets from the cabin of an officer, where she had remained unnoticed during the general confusion occasioned by the ship running aground. Even the princesses appropriated trifles whenever they had an opportunity. Our experience, however, proves that the lessons they have received from their Christian pastors on the disgracefulness of theft have had a practically good effect.

Neither can I deny that the morals of the Tahaitians were very exceptionable in another point, in which also the influence of the Missionaries has been beneficially exerted. If the modesty which conceals the mysteries of love among civilized nations be the offspring only of their intellectual culture, it is not surprising that a wholly uninstructed people should be insensible to such a feeling, and in its unconsciousness should even have established public solemnities which would strike us as excessively indelicate.

The coarse hospitality of the Tahaitians went so far as to present to a welcome guest, a sister, a daughter, or even a wife; and they have been known to sell them for pearls, pieces of glass, or implements of iron. The women who distributed their favours indiscriminately, were almost always of the lowest class; but a most licentious association called Ehrioi, including both sexes, existed among the higher. Renouncing matrimony, and the hopes of progeny, its members rambled about the island leading the most dissolute lives; and if a child was born among them, the laws of the society compelled its murder, or the expulsion of the mother. The men were all warriors, and stood in high estimation among the people. The Ehrioi themselves were proud of the title, and even the King O Tu belonged to this profligate institution, to which, fortunately, the Missionaries have put an end.

Where such manners prevailed, and woman was regarded merely as an object of pleasure, she could not stand in very high estimation; and love, in its best sense, remained wholly unknown among them. Hence the women of Tahaiti, although not so much secluded as among many other nations, were not permitted to eat with the men, and when the King and the Royal Family visited Cook, on board his ship, he was obliged to entertain even the princesses in a separate cabin.

The fidelity of a wife among the Tahaitians required that she should not favour any man without the knowledge and consent of her husband; and a beating was the punishment generally incurred by a violation of this duty.

Among the failings of the Tahaitians, their love of the intoxicating liquor which they prepared from the much cultivated Ava root, must not be omitted. Nor have the Missionaries been wholly unsuccessful in this respect. The drink is no longer allowed to be prepared, nor even the root to be cultivated; but unfortunately, its place has been partly supplied by the introduction of our wine and brandy; we, however, never saw a drunken person.

Having now noticed all that was reprehensible in the otherwise amiable character of the Ante-christian Tahaitian, I hope the reader, in consideration of his many good qualities, will forgive his faults, and, in a friendly disposition towards him, cast a glance upon his innocent amusements, which were chiefly derived from music, dancing, mock-fights, and theatrical representations.

Their musical instruments were very simple, and of two kinds only: the one, a sort of flute, producing four notes, and blown with the nostrils; the other, a drum, made of the hollow trunk of a tree; but the accompanying songs, usually extempore poems, were pretty, and showed the delicacy of their ear. The girls excelled in the dance; the married women were forbidden to take part in it, and the men never did. The dancers executed a species of ballet, and, according to the judgment of travellers, they might with little trouble become capable of performing on our theatres. The English dances they soon learnt, and in the well-known hornpipe, especially, displayed much grace.

The mock-fights were of course in imitation of their serious warfare, and they parried with admirable dexterity the blow of a club or thrust of a lance, by which otherwise they must have been severely wounded. The dramatic pieces were performed by both sexes, and sometimes by persons of the highest quality. They were of a mixed character, serious, and comic, but for want of a thorough acquaintance with the language, they have been very imperfectly described to us. Thus, oppressed by no care, burdened by no toil, tormented by no passion, seldom visited by sickness, their wants easily satisfied, and their pleasures often recurring, the Tahaitians passed a life of enjoyment under the magnificent sky of the tropics, and amid scenes worthy of Paradise.

On the 12th of March, a beautiful bright morning, we had the pleasure to perceive Tahaiti before us, like a light cloud in the clear horizon. All that we had read of its loveliness now rose to our remembrance, heightened by the vivid colouring of the imagination; but seventy miles were yet to be traversed ere we could tread the land of expectation, and a very slow progress, occasioned by a flagging wind, tried our patience. We continued, however, to advance, and the light cloud became larger, and denser, and higher, soon assuming the appearance of three separate hills belonging to different islands; the highest point, eight thousand feet above the level of the sea, is the summit of a mountain, distinguished from the others by its conical form.

We next recognized the large rugged masses of rock of the interior, which have a most romantic appearance. The country gradually unfolded all its charms; the luxuriant growth of the trees, even to the mountains' tops, reminded us of the scenery of Brazil, and the picturesque valleys, with their thickets of bread-fruit, orange, and cocoa-trees, their cultivated fields, and plantations of bananas, became at length distinctly visible.

It was not till the 14th that we reached the Cape, called by Cook Cape Venus, because he there observed the transit of this planet over the sun; and from its beauty, it deserves to be named after the charming goddess herself. It is a low narrow tongue of land, running out northward from the island, thickly shadowed by cocoa-trees, and forming, by its curve, the harbour of Matarai, not a very secure one, but generally preferred by sailors on account of the celebrity bestowed on it by Cook.

When we were still a few miles distant from Cape Venus, we fired a gun to draw attention to the flag hoisted at the fore-mast, as a signal for a pilot. We soon saw a European boat steering towards us; it brought us a pilot, who, to our great surprise, addressed us in the Russian language, having recognized our flag as belonging to that nation: he was an Englishman of the name of Williams, who had first been a sailor on board a merchant ship, afterwards entered the service of the Russian American Company on the north-west coast of America, and was at length settled for life in Tahaiti. His wife was a native of the island; he was the father of a family, and carried on the occupation of a pilot in the Bay of Matarai. Wanderers of this kind often settle in the islands of the South Sea; but while they bring with them many vices peculiar to the lower classes in civilized life, are generally too ignorant and rough to produce any favourable influence on the natives. They are not all liable to this censure; and of about twenty English and Americans whom I found so naturalized in Tahaiti, some assuredly do not deserve it.

Having a pilot on board, we steered direct for the extreme point of Cape Venus, where floated the national standard of Tahaiti. This flag displays a white star in a field of red, and, like many of the present arrangements, owes its origin to the Missionaries, who do not indeed bear the title of Kings of the island, but exercise an unlimited influence over the minds of the natives. We passed safely by the shallows lying before the Matawai Bay, (upon which Captain Wallis grounded, and which he called, after his ship, the Dolphin,) round the headland, to the western side, and at last anchored opposite the village of Matawai, at a distance of two hundred fathoms from the shore, in a black clay bottom of fifteen fathoms depth.

Our frigate, as it entered the Bay, attracted to the beach a crowd of curious gazers, who greeted our arrival with a shout of joy. Numerous boats laden with all kinds of fruits, provisions, and other articles of merchandize, immediately put off from the shore, and we were soon surrounded by gay and noisy Tahaitians. As soon as the sails were taken in, I gave them permission to come on board, of which they eagerly availed themselves. With their wares on their backs, they climbed merrily up the sides of the ship, and the deck was soon transformed into a busy market, where all was frolic and fun; the goods were offered with a jest, and the bargains concluded with laughter. In a short time each Tahaitian had selected a Russian associate, to whom, with a fraternal embrace, he tendered his wish to exchange names,—a ceremony which implied a pledge to surrender to the new friend whatever he might wish for.

It is probable that these sudden attachments were not quite disinterested; a view of procuring a better barter for their goods might have had some effect in producing the zeal with which they were struck up; but they certainly had every appearance of sincerity and cordiality, and in less than an hour these friendly allies were seen walking in couples, arm in arm, about the deck, as though they had been acquainted for years.

Our clothing appeared to be prized by the Tahaitians above every thing we offered them, and the possession of any article of this kind set them leaping, as if out of their wits, for joy. On this day we saw no females; and when we were afterwards occasionally visited by the women, they always behaved with the greatest propriety.

When the sun declined, our new acquaintances left us to return to their homes, satisfied with their bargains, and delighted with the presents they had received, and without having stolen any thing, although above a hundred of them had been on board at once.

I had sent a message to the Missionary Wilson, by an officer who now returned, bringing for answer an assurance that the Missionary would with pleasure do all in his power to assist us in procuring our supplies; a promise he faithfully kept.

On the following morning we were greeted by the sun from a cloudless sky, with a most superb illumination of the country opposite to his rising. His rays glittering on the mountain-tops before they reached our horizon, gradually enlivened the variegated green that clothed their sides down to the vales, till the King of Day burst upon our sight in all his splendour, arraying the luxuriant landscape of the shore in still more enchanting beauty. Among the thickets of fruit-trees were seen the dwellings of the happy inhabitants of this great pleasure-ground, built of bamboos, and covered with large leaves, standing each in its little garden; but, to our great astonishment, the stillness of death reigned among them; and even when the sun stood high in the heavens, no one was to be seen.

The warm friendships formed but yesterday seemed already to have cooled; we were quite forgotten. At length we obtained from the boat, sent off to us at break of day with provisions, an explanation of this enigma. The inhabitants of Tahaiti were celebrating the Sunday, on which account they did not leave their houses, where they lay on their bellies reading the Bible and howling aloud; laying aside every species of occupation, they devoted, as they said, the whole day to prayer. According to our reckoning, the day was Saturday. This difference proceeded from the first Missionaries having reached Tahaiti from the west by the way of New Holland, while we had come eastward by Cape Horn.

I resolved to go ashore and pay a visit to Mr. Wilson, that I might procure, through his means, a convenient place for our astronomical observations. We landed at the point of the Cape, because the shade of a thick palm grove there offered us immediate protection. No one received us on the strand; no human being, not even a dog, was visible. The very birds seemed here to celebrate the Sunday by silence, unless, indeed, it was somewhat too hot for singing. A little brook, meandering among shrubs and flowers, alone took the liberty of mingling its murmurs with the devotions of the Tahaitians. I sauntered along a narrow trodden path under the shade of palms, bananas, orange, and lemon-trees, inhaling their fragrance, and delighting in the luxuriance of nature. Though beautiful as this country is, it does not equal Brazil in the variety of its productions, and in the numbers of its humming-birds and butterflies. The loud prayer of the Tahaitian Christians reached my ears, as I approached their habitations. All the doors were closed, and not even the children allowed to enjoy the beauty of the morning.

The small but pleasant house of the Missionary, built after the European fashion, stands in the midst of a kitchen-garden richly provided with all kinds of European vegetables.

Mr. Wilson gave me a cordial welcome to his neat and simple dwelling, and presented to me his wife, an Englishwoman, and two children, besides two Englishmen, whom he named as Messrs. Bennet and Tyrman. They belonged to the London Missionary Society, and had left England three years before to visit the Missionary Settlements in the South Sea.

The chief Missionary, to whom the others are subordinate, is named Nott, and lives in the capital where the King resides. He is now far advanced in life. He has made himself master of the Tahaitian language, and was the first who ever wrote it. He has translated the Bible, a Prayer Book, and some Hymns; and has printed a Grammar of the language, under the title of, "A Grammar of the Tahaitian Dialect of the Polynesian Language. Tahaiti: printed at the Mission Press, Burder's Point, 1823."

He also first instructed the Tahaitians in reading and writing, which acquirements are now tolerably common among them. I am sorry not to have known Mr. Nott better, and therefore not to have it in my power to judge of the man as well as the Missionary. His character stands very high. Wilson, also an old man, has now lived twenty years in Tahaiti; he was originally a common sailor, but has zealously devoted himself to theology, and is honest and good-natured. Including Nott and Wilson, there are six Missionaries in Tahaiti alone, and only four among all the other Society Islands. Each Missionary possesses a piece of land, cultivated by the natives, which produces him in superfluity all that he requires, and he also receives an annual allowance of fifty pounds from the London Missionary Society. This Society has also sent Missionaries to Tongatabu, one of the Friendly Islands, and to Nukashiva, lately made known to us by Krusenstern.

Besides these English Missionaries, some native Tahaitians, after receiving a suitable education, are sent to spread Christianity among the islands of the dangerous Archipelago. In Russia, a careful education and diligent study at schools and universities is necessary to qualify any one to be a teacher of religion. The London Missionary Society is more easily satisfied; a half savage, confused by the dogmas of an uneducated sailor, is, according to them, perfectly fitted for the sacred office.

It was now church-time, and Wilson requested me to be present at the service,—an invitation which I accepted with pleasure. A broad straight path, planted with the cocoa and lofty bread-fruit tree, leads from his house, about a ten minutes' walk, to the place of worship. The church-yard, with its black wooden crosses, impresses the mind with a feeling of solemnity: the church itself is a handsome building, about twenty fathoms long and ten broad, constructed of light wood-work adapted to the climate, and whitened on the outside, which gives it a pretty effect among the green shades that surround it. The numerous large windows remain unglazed, because a free admission of the air is here desirable in all seasons; the roof, made of ingeniously plaited reeds, and covered with immense leaves, is a sufficient defence against the heaviest rain; there is neither steeple nor clock. The interior of the church is one large hall, the walls of which are neatly kept; it is filled with a number of benches, so placed, in long rows, that the occupants can have a convenient view of the pulpit in the centre. When we entered, the church was full even to crowding, the men seated on one side, and the women on the other; they almost all had psalm-books lying before them; the most profound stillness reigned in the assembly. Near the pulpit, which Wilson mounted, was placed a bench for Messrs. Bennet and Tyrman, on which I also took my seat.

Notwithstanding the seriousness and devotion apparent among the Tahaitians, it is almost impossible for an European, seeing them for the first time in their Sunday attire, to refrain from laughter. The high value which they set on clothes of our manufacture has already been remarked; they are more proud of possessing them than are our ladies of diamonds and Persian shawls, or our gentlemen of stars and orders. As they know nothing of our fashions, they pay no sort of attention to the cut, and even age and wear do not much diminish their estimation of their attire; a ripped-out seam, or a hole, is no drawback in the elegance of the article. These clothes, which are brought to Tahaiti by merchant-ships, are purchased at a rag-market, and sold here at an enormous profit. The Tahaitian therefore, finding a complete suit of clothes very expensive, contents himself with a single garment; whoever can obtain an English military coat, or even a plain one, goes about with the rest of his body naked, except the universally-worn girdle; the happy owner of a waistcoat or a pair of trowsers, thinks his wardrobe amply furnished. Some have nothing more than a shirt, and others, as much oppressed by the heat under a heavy cloth mantle as they would be in a Russian bath, are far too vain of their finery to lay it aside. Shoes, boots, or stockings, are rarely met with, and the coats, mostly too tight and too short, make the oddest appearance imaginable; many of their wearers can scarcely move their arms, and are forced to stretch them out like the sails of a windmill, while their elbows, curious to see the world, peep through slits in the seams. Let any one imagine such an assembly, perfectly satisfied of the propriety of their costume, and wearing, to complete the comic effect, a most ultra-serious expression of countenance, and he will easily believe that it was impossible for me to be very devout in their presence. The attire of the females, though not quite so absurd, was by no means picturesque; some wore white, or striped men's shirts, which did not conceal their knees, and others were wrapped in sheets. Their hair was cut quite close to the roots, according to a fashion introduced by the Missionaries, and their heads covered by little European chip hats of a most tasteless form, and decorated with ribbons and flowers, made in Tahaiti. But the most valuable article of dress was a coloured gown, an indubitable sign of the possessor's opulence, and the object of her unbounded vanity.

When Wilson first mounted the pulpit, he bent his head forward, and concealing his face with an open Bible, prayed in silence; the whole congregation immediately imitated him, using their Psalm-books instead of Bibles. After this, the appointed psalm was sung to a most incongruous tune, every voice being exerted to its utmost pitch, in absolute defiance of harmony. Wilson then read some chapters from the Bible, the congregation kneeling twice during the intervals; the greater part of them appeared very attentive, and the most decorous silence reigned, which was, however, occasionally interrupted by the chattering and tittering of some young girls seated behind me. I observed that some threatening looks directed towards them by Messrs. Bennet and Tyrman, seemed to silence them for a moment, but their youthful spirits soon overcoming their fears, the whispering and giggling recommenced, and glances were cast at the white stranger, which seemed to intimate no unwillingness to commence a closer acquaintance. After the conclusion of the sermon, another psalm was sung, and the service concluded. The display of costume, as the congregation strolled homewards in groups, with the greatest self-complacency, through the beautiful broad avenue, their psalm-books under their arms, was still more strikingly ludicrous than in church. I had by this time, however, lost all inclination to laugh.

I had assisted at a great religious assembly of the new, devoted, so called Christian Tahaitians; and the comparison naturally arising in my mind, between what I had seen and the descriptions of the early travellers, had introduced reflections which became less and less agreeable, in proportion as I acquired a greater insight into the recent history of the island.

After many fruitless efforts, some English Missionaries succeeded at length, in the year 1797, in introducing what they called Christianity into Tahaiti, and even in gaining over to their doctrine the King Tajo, who then governed the whole island in peace and tranquillity. This conversion was a spark thrown into a powder magazine, and was followed by a fearful explosion. The Marais were suddenly destroyed by order of the King—every memorial of the former worship defaced—the new religion forcibly established, and whoever would not adopt it, put to death. With the zeal for making proselytes, the rage of tigers took possession of a people once so gentle. Streams of blood flowed—whole races were exterminated; many resolutely met the death they preferred to the renunciation of their ancient faith. Some few escaped by flight to the recesses of the lofty mountains, where they still live in seclusion, faithful to the gods of their ancestors. Schiller's exclamation—"*Furchtbar ist der Mensch in seinem wahn,*" was dreadfully confirmed.

Ambition associated itself, as usual, to fanaticism. King Tajo, not content with seeing in the remains of his people none but professors of the new faith, resolved on making conquests that he might force it on the other Society Islands. He had already succeeded with most of them, when a young warrior, Pomareh, King of the little island of Tabua, took the field against him. What he wanted in numbers was supplied by his unexampled valour, and his superiority in the art of war.

He subdued one island after another, and at last Tahaiti itself, and having captured its King, offered the zealot murderer of his innocent subjects as a sacrifice to their manes. In the end, he subjected to his sceptre all the islands which had hitherto remained independent, and as sovereign of the whole Archipelago, took up his residence in Tahaiti. He left to the conquered Kings the government of their islands, requiring from them a yearly tribute in pigs and fruits; and to consolidate his dominion by family connexion, he married a daughter of the most powerful of these royal vassals, her three sisters, according to an ancient custom, becoming at the same time his wives.

Peace was thus restored to Tahaiti and the whole Archipelago. Pomareh was a wise and mild ruler. He left his subjects undisturbed in their new religion, although he did not profess it himself. The Missionaries, now limited to their powers of persuasion, found means to retain their disciples in their adopted faith, so that the refugees of the mountains preferred remaining in their retreats, to finding themselves objects of hatred and contempt amongst their old friends and relations. At length Pomareh himself, with his whole family, yielded to the arguments of the Missionary Nott, allowed himself to be baptized, and died as a Christian, in the prime of life, in consequence of an immoderate indulgence in the spirituous liquors which he had obtained from the ships of his new brethren.

An unconquerable passion for ardent spirits had acquired an entire dominion over him, although he was so well aware of their deleterious effects, as to have often exclaimed, when under the influence of intoxication, "O King, to-day could thy fat swine govern better than thou canst!" This weakness was, however, so much over-balanced by his many good qualities, his well-tried valour, his inflexible justice, his constant mildness and generosity, that he possessed to the last the universal esteem and love of his subjects, by whom his loss was still deplored when we arrived at Tahaiti, almost two years after his death, although he had reigned as an unlimited monarch, and they now possessed a constitution resembling, or rather aping, that of England. This had been introduced by the influence of the Missionaries, whose power over the minds of the Tahaitians is unbounded; they had persuaded the people to adopt it during the minority of Pomareh's son, a child of four years old at the period of our visit; but from the general regret with which the days of the absolute King were remembered, it did not appear to have given much satisfaction.

According to this Constitution, Tahaiti is divided into nineteen districts, and the neighbouring island of Eimeo, having no especial viceroy, into eight. Every district has its governor and its judge, whose business is to settle disputes and maintain order. The first is appointed by the Parliament, and the latter elected by the people. These nominations are for one year only—but may be renewed at the expiration of the term. Important affairs are submitted to the Parliament, which, consisting of deputies from all the provinces, possesses the legislative, as the King does the executive power.

The Tahaitians, accustomed to a blind reverence for the Missionaries, consult them in all their undertakings, and by means of the Constitution have so confirmed their power, both as priests and rulers, that it would be difficult for governor, judge, or member of parliament, to retain their offices after having incurred their displeasure. They have shown their artful policy in the choice of a guardian for the young King. It has fallen on the tributary King of the island of Balabola, distinguished by his giant height of seven feet, and by his enormous corpulence, which almost prevents his moving, but by no mental qualification.

This mountain of flesh, that at a distance might rather be taken for some unknown monster than for a man, naturally finds it more convenient to his indolence to be merely the mouthpiece of the Missionaries, and that their dominion may also be secured for the future, Mr. Nott has the sole charge of the young monarch's education, and will not fail to bring him up in the habit of implicit obedience.

The actual document securing the Constitution had not yet appeared; the Missionaries were still employed on it, well convinced, that whatever they should insert would be received without opposition. When complete, it will probably issue in due form from their Printing-Office, and will be interesting, if some future traveller should bring us the translation.

Firm as the foundation of the Missionaries' power appeared, one little cloud was visible in the political firmament. A son of the vanquished King

Tajo yet existed, and was not entirely without adherents. If by any chance he should succeed in gaining possession of the throne, he might remember that these men had assisted in excluding him from it. For this reason, they resolved to confirm the title of the young Pomareh, by a solemn coronation; and to strengthen his party, all the tributary princes of the whole Archipelago were invited to be present at the ceremony.

The preparations for this solemnity had long been carrying on, and as it was now soon to take place, nearly all the kings, with numerous suites, had arrived in Tahaiti. Among them was the powerful ruler of Ulietea, the grandfather of the infant sovereign; he had brought with him several hundred warriors, many of them armed with muskets.

We wished much to have been present at this first coronation of a King of the Society Islands; but as our time would not permit it, I obtained from Mr. Tyrman an account of the order and plan of the ceremony.

The kings, princes, members of parliament, and other high officers, were to assemble at the residence of the Queen, and thence in a regular procession, arranged according to their several ranks and dignities, and headed by the young King and the Missionaries, to pass to an appointed open space, where a throne of stone had been erected, on which the little Pomareh was to be seated. The procession was then to form a circle round him, and Mr. Tyrman, after making a speech, was to set on the King's head a crown, resembling in shape that of England, in which country it had been made. A Bible was then to be placed in his hand, with the admonition, "According to this Law, thou shall govern thy people." Upon this, the train being marshalled as before, the King should descend from his throne, and proceed to the church, where, after the performance of divine service, he should be anointed. The ceremonies should then conclude with a grand banquet.

It is remarkable that the Bible, and not the Act of the Constitution, was to be given to the King, as the rule of his government. Was not a sly mental reservation perhaps intended by this? If the Constitution should not have exactly the effect intended, and the Tahaitians, emboldened by it, should seek to withdraw themselves from their leading-strings, then might the pupil of Nott, bound to them by no oath, come forward to them boldly, and force them back under the yoke of the Missionaries; all the while conscientiously obeying the rule of conduct which had been delivered to him, according to the interpretation he had been taught to put on it.

How this coronation turned out—whether the son of Tajo allowed it to pass quietly—whether he has met the fate of many an unfortunate European pretender, or survives to become the originator of a civil war, which may yet give another destiny to Tahaiti, remains to be learnt from the accounts of some future traveller.

Religion and political institutions may raise a nation in a short period to a high point of civilization, and they may also serve, as in case of the Turks, to retain them in perpetual barbarism. How will these mighty powers operate on the Tahaitians? How can they, the qualifications of their authors considered!

True, genuine Christianity, and a liberal government, might have soon given to this people, endowed by nature with the seeds of every social virtue, a rank among civilized nations. Under such a blessed influence, the arts and sciences would soon have taken root, the intellect of the people would have expanded, and a just estimation of all that is good, beautiful, and eternally true, would have refined their manners and ennobled their hearts. Europe would soon have admired, perhaps have envied Tahaiti: but the religion taught by the Missionaries is not true Christianity, though it may possibly comprehend some of its doctrines, but half understood even by the teachers themselves. That it was established by force, is of itself an evidence against its Christian principle. A religion which consists in the eternal repetition of prescribed prayers, which forbids every innocent pleasure, and cramps or annihilates every mental power, is a libel on the Divine Founder of Christianity, the benign Friend of human-kind. It is true, that the religion of the Missionaries has, with a great deal of evil, effected some good. It has abolished heathen superstitions, and an irrational worship, but it has introduced new errors in their stead. It has restrained the vices of theft and incontinence, but it has given birth to bigotry, hypocrisy, and a hatred and contempt of all other modes of faith, which was once foreign to the open and benevolent character of the Tahaitian. It has put and end to avowed human sacrifices, but many more human beings have been actually sacrificed to it, than ever were to their heathen gods.

The elder Forster estimated, as we have already seen, the population of Tahaiti at one hundred and thirty thousand souls. Allowing that he over-calculated it, by even as much as fifty thousand, still eighty thousand remained:—the present population amounts to only eight thousand; so that nine-tenths must have disappeared. The diseases introduced by the ardent spirits, the manufacture of Europe and America, may, indeed, have much increased the mortality, but they are also known in many islands in the South Seas, without having caused any perceptible diminution in the population. It is not known that plague of any kind has ever raged here: it was, therefore, the bloody persecution instigated by the Missionaries which performed the office of a desolating infection. I really believe that these pious people were themselves shocked at the consequences of their zeal; but they soon consoled themselves; and have ever since continued to watch with the most vigilant severity over the maintenance of every article of their faith. Hence, among the remains of these murdered people, their former admirable industry, and their joyous buoyancy of spirits, have been changed for continual praying, and meditating upon things which the teachers understand as little as the taught.

The Tahaitians of the present day hardly know how to plait their mats, make their paper stuffs, or cultivate a few roots. They content themselves with the bread-fruit, which the soil yields spontaneously in quantities more than sufficient for their reduced population. Their navy, which excited the astonishment of Europeans, has entirely disappeared. They build no vessels but a few little paltry canoes, with which they fish off the neighbouring coral islands, and make their longest voyages in American and European boats which they have purchased. With the method of producing those commodities of civilized nations which they prize so highly, they are still as much as ever unacquainted. They possess sheep, and excellent cotton; but no spinning-wheel, no loom, has yet been set in motion among them; they choose rather to buy their cloth and cotton of foreigners for real gold and pearls; one of our sailors sold an old shirt for five piastres. Horses and cattle have been brought to them, but the few that remain have fallen into the possession of strangers, and have become so scarce, that one hundred piastres was asked for an ox, that we wanted in provisioning the ship. The Queen alone possesses a pair of horses, but she never uses them. The island contains but one smith, though the assistance of the forge and bellows would be so useful in repairing the iron tools which have superseded those of stone formerly in use. It is extraordinary that even the foreigners established here carry on no kind of mechanical trade. Can it be that the Missionaries object to it? It is certain that they possess great influence even over the settlers. An American, however, was planning the introduction of a sugar manufactory, and promised himself great profit from it.

By order of the Missionaries, the flute, which once awakened innocent pleasure, is heard no more. No music but that of the psalms is suffered in Tahaiti: dancing, mock-fights, and dramatic representations are no longer permitted. Every pleasure is punished as a sin, among a people whom Nature destined to the most cheerful enjoyment. One of our friends having begun to sing for joy over a present he had received, was immediately asked by his comrades, with great terror, what he thought would be the consequence, should the Missionaries hear of it.

It is remarkable that the degenerate Tahaitians are no longer even in person such as they are described by the early travellers. Their religion appears to have had an effect inimical to their beauty. The large-grown Yeris, solely employed in praying, eating, and sleeping, are all, men and women, excessively fat even in early youth. The smaller common people, constrained to some degree of industry, look plump and well fed, but not so swollen as their superiors, and more fine forms are therefore to be seen among them than among the Yeris: the latter also frequently suffer under a most disfiguring disease caused by want of exercise and excess of nourishment: the legs swell to such a degree from the knees downward, that the form of the calf and foot is entirely lost, and the thick cylinders which usurp the place of legs, and from under which the toes only project, resemble nothing but the legs of elephants; thence the name of elephantism has been bestowed on the complaint by Europeans. It does not appear to cause much pain.

The men of both classes shave the beard, and both sexes cut their hair so close, that the skin can be seen under it; a fashion ugly enough for any face, but especially so with their brown complexions, as it gives them an ape-like appearance. As, however, a compliance with this custom, is a mark of Christianity, and the heathen fugitives to the mountains have retained their long hair, even the young females are proud of thus disfiguring themselves.

All vanity is sin, and all care of the person is vanity. Hence the fat Yeri beauties no longer shelter their skins from the burning rays of the sun, and are become as brown as the rest. All the graces have departed from them; their fascinating smiles have vanished; and the rancid cocoa-oil with which they smear themselves may be smelt at many paces distance. In short, either the picture drawn of them by the early travellers was a monstrous flattery, or they are altogether different from what they were. I saw but one handsome girl at Tahaiti; she was the sister of the little King, only fourteen years old, and already the bride of her uncle, the Prince of Ulietea. The men far surpass the women both in form and feature.

The Missionaries have abolished the custom of tattooing, and so far at least spared the Tahaitians some useless torment. These marks are now only to be seen on people of the middle age and upwards—never on the young. The first voyagers who visited this island, describe the tattooing as representing half-moons, birds, and irregular or zig-zag lines; but on a better acquaintance with Europeans, the fashion changed, and drawings of our tools, animals, and even compasses and mathematical instruments, were executed with the greatest exactness on their bodies. Pantaloons being articles in particular request among them, he who could not obtain a pair, comforted himself by having the representation of them etched on his legs. Many of these are still to be seen.

We much wished to have had an opportunity of comparing the *soi-disant* Christian Tahaitians, with the heathen inhabitants of the mountains; but it would have taken too much time to seek them out in their retreats, which they leave only at night for the purpose of robbing the dwellers in the valleys, among whom they dare not appear in the day.

If the religion of the Missionaries has neither tended to enlighten the Tahaitians nor to render them happy, just as little can be expected from the Constitution founded upon it, which seems adapted only to draw yet tighter the bonds in which this amiable people are held by their zealous converters, and to retain them wholly under their authority.

By the influence of Wilson, a small house situated on Cape Venus was cleared for our astronomical observations: we were told it stood precisely on the same spot where Cook's Observatory had formerly been erected. As a particular favour from the Government, I was also accommodated with a royal pleasure-house in its neighbourhood for my private residence. This very large building, which resembled an ancient temple in appearance, had been a favourite abode of the deceased monarch Pomareh, and since his death had remained uninhabited, out of respect for his memory. A number of utensils which had belonged to him, and a canoe, on which he had obtained many splendid victories, were still preserved here as memorials of the beloved king. The house was wholly without walls—the roof of leaves resting on numerous pillars; a mode of construction extremely well adapted to this warm and dry climate. The environs were very beautiful: high trees covered with thickest foliage invited to repose under their shadows, and a brook clear as crystal offered an inviting bath. The air was filled with the perfume of a neighbouring orange-grove, which scattered its fruit upon the earth. The lemons and oranges, which we found delicious, the Tahaitians despised as too common. Since I could only afford to remain a very short time at Tahaiti, Dr. Eschscholz and myself immediately took possession of my new abode, and erected our little observatory. After a long, wearisome voyage, I cannot express the delight I experienced in reposing amidst such enchanting scenes of natural beauty. We passed a charming evening, and a most refreshing night under our roof of leaves.

In the morning, as we were drinking our coffee and smoking our pipes, while laying the plan of our observations so as to employ our short time to the best advantage, a messenger arrived from the Queen requesting to speak with me.

I desired he might be admitted, and a giant Yen strode proudly in, accompanied by our pilot as interpreter. His only garment, with the exception of the girdle always worn by the men, was an old worn-out sand-coloured coat, with great shining buttons, in the fashion of the last century, and so much too small for its present possessor, that he could not button it, while his naked arms stuck out more than a quarter of a yard below the sleeves. His bald head was covered by a red night-cap, which, to show his knowledge of the customs of civilized nations, he raised a little on his entrance.

He uttered, as he came towards me, the word Jorona (good day), stretched out his great hand to me, and then, without waiting for my invitation, seated himself on the ground close to my feet, with his legs crossed in the Turkish fashion. The Queen had sent him to inform me, that she was curious to see the Commander of a Russian frigate, and would gladly have entertained me at her court; but as she feared I would not absent myself so long from Matarai, she had resolved to pay me a visit accompanied by the whole Royal Family. The ambassador added, that these exalted personages, who had travelled by water, would soon arrive, and that he must hasten to receive them; then rising, he pressed my hand, repeated his jorona, touched his night-cap, and disappeared.

I had scarcely time to prepare for the reception of my illustrious guests, when the concourse of people hastening to the shore announced their approach. A man soon appeared as *avant courier*, in the short, red uniform-jacket of an English drummer, an uncommonly showy, many-coloured girdle, and the rest of his body, according to custom, quite naked. His legs were adorned by a tattooed representation of pantaloons; and when he turned his back and stooped very little, he showed also a drawing of a large compass, with all the two-and-thirty points executed with striking exactness. In his hand he held a rusty broad-sword, and on his head was proudly displayed an old torn three-cornered hat, with a long red feather. Our interpreter described him as the royal Master of the Ceremonies; but it afterwards appeared, that though not apparently belonging to the Yens, but to the smaller race, he held several other offices in conjunction with this— those of cook and chamberlain, for example: his talent, however, seemed most to incline to that of court-fool or harlequin.

In all his motions, gestures and grimaces, he displayed so singular a vivacity, that he might have been considered insane. Without the least ceremony, or paying the slightest attention to me, he took possession of my whole house. Several servants, in the livery of nature, followed him with the various articles necessary to the convenience of the Royal visitors. He immediately ordered that the whole floor should be covered with matting, and had every thing placed as he thought proper, leaping about all the while with both feet in the air, as if his life depended on the velocity of his motions. No one of the servants pleased him; his tongue ran incessantly; and his sword was flourished about in all directions.

His preparations were not yet complete, when we saw a long procession of Tahaitians approach, two and two, bearing on their shoulders various kinds of provisions fastened on bamboo poles. This set our caperer upon increased activity. Two or three springs having carried him out of the house, he commanded the bearers to set down their burdens, which were presents from the Queen to me, in a certain order, in front of my dwelling. Three large pigs formed the right flank; and opposite to them were piled potatoes, yams, sweet potatoes, and all kinds of delicious fruit. When the Master of the Ceremonies had arranged them all to his satisfaction, he turned, for the first time, to me, and endeavoured, with many comical pantomimic gestures, to make me understand that all were mine. At length the Queen herself appeared, followed by a numerous train of attendants. She walked first, carrying the little King in her arms, and holding her daughter, the betrothed of the Prince of Ulietea, by the hand. After her came her three sisters, all like herself, large fat women, and then the whole crowd of the Court. The rear was brought up by a multitude of people of the lower class, bearing viands for the Royal entertainment, in utensils made of various kinds of gourds. Among the dainties was a live pig, which squeaking and grunting in anticipation of its fate, supplied to this orderly procession the absence of a musical band.

The Queen and her three sisters were wrapped in sheets; and their straw hats still bore streamers of black crape, as signs of mourning for the late King. The little Pomareh, a pretty, lively boy, was dressed quite in the European fashion, in a jacket and trowsers of bombasin; he wore a round hat, but his feet, like those of all the other Tahaitians, were bare. They object that any kind of shoe hinders their walking. The young bride, a handsome girl, as I have before said, was very lightly clad in a short striped shirt, without any covering on her head. The giant Yeris who formed the Court, mostly wore white shirts, and round straw hats with black ribbons.

It was the first time, since the death of her consort, that the Queen had entered these precincts, and a shower of tears fell from her eyes at the remembrance of the past. The whole court, as in duty bound, was also immediately dissolved in grief; but this sorrowful mood did not last long; their faces gradually cleared up—the Queen dried her tears, and greeted me kindly. The Master of the Ceremonies then conducted the Royal Family to the best mats, on which they sat down in the Asiatic fashion. One of my chairs was placed opposite the Royal Family, and I was invited to take my seat. In the mean time, the Master of the Ceremonies had vanished to prepare the repast.

When the Queen, after surveying me from head to foot, had communicated her remarks and opinions to the company, I requested the interpreter to thank her, in my name, for my friendly reception on the island—for the presents she had made me, and for the high honour conferred on me in this visit. She received my thanks very graciously, and ordered some questions to be put me, which I answered with all due respect. She inquired how old I was?—whether my voyage had been long?—whether I was a Christian?—and how often I prayed *daily*? This last question afforded me an opportunity, had I thought fit, to give her Majesty some new ideas on the subject of the Missionary religion; but I did not feel myself quite capable of entering into a theological dispute, and therefore merely replied, that Christianity taught us, that we should be judged according to our actions rather than the number of our prayers. I do not know how the interpreter rendered my answer, or whether the Queen considered me as a heretic, but this I conjectured, from her speaking no more on religious subjects, and asking me, in order to change the conversation, whether the earth were really round? I assured her Majesty that I could answer from my own experience, as I was now sailing round it for the third time. This appeared to excite some astonishment; but my assertion concerning its spherical form still gained but small credit.

I then produced some presents for the Queen, her family, and their immediate attendants, which, though in themselves extremely trifling, were received with great pleasure, and produced a degree of hilarity little consistent with the symbols of mourning worn by the Royal party, or the feelings they had displayed on their first arrival.

To the Queen I presented a piece of calico four or five yards long, a coloured silk handkerchief, a small looking-glass, a pair of scissors, and some glass beads; to the young Princess, a silk handkerchief, beads, and a looking-glass; to the sisters of the Queen, cotton handkerchiefs, glasses, and scissors; their attendants, among whom were four ladies, were content with knives.

During this time the Master of the Ceremonies had killed the pig, and baked it in the earth in the Tahaitian manner. As soon as the Royal Family had resumed their seats he brought it in, and placed it before the Queen, on a great banana-leaf, other servants spreading yams, potatoes, and bread-fruit upon the ground. My chair was brought and placed opposite to the Queen, who invited me, with much friendliness, to partake of the meal. I preferred, however, being an idle spectator, for it was still very early in the day, and I had no appetite. When all the provisions were brought in, the Master of the Ceremonies made a leap into the air, flourished his rusty broad-sword, and then repeated a loud prayer. All the company hung down their heads, and prayed with him in silence. The prayer being concluded, the Master of the Ceremonies seized the baked pig by the hind-legs and tore it in two; then, having carved the whole with his broad-sword, laid a tolerably large portion on leaves before each member of the Royal Family, who immediately attacked it with a good appetite, helping themselves with fingers and teeth, instead of knife and fork. During the repast, the suite ate nothing, but remained looking on, and I did not perceive that they were indemnified for their abstinence, even when the residue of the feast was carried out. When the repast was over, and a prayer said as before, the Royal personages washed their hands with water, and their mouths with cocoa-milk, and then lay down altogether to sleep; the attendants retiring. I offered to her Majesty the use of my bed, which she condescendingly accepted; and during the siesta, I returned to my plans for our astronomical observations. On awaking, the Queen expressed a wish to see my frigate; my time was not at my own disposal, but I entrusted to one of my officers the charge of doing the honours of the ship to our Royal guests, as well as circumstances would permit. On leaving me, the Queen pressed my hand in the most friendly manner, and repeated her jorona several times; her whole train followed her.

On the strand, according to the account of my officer, the canoes lay in readiness for the excursion. The Queen, accompanied by her family and our officer, put off in her own European boat; the Master of the Ceremonies took his station in the fore-part of the boat, turning his compass to the company, and continued, during the passage, his ridiculous harlequinades with his limbs and broad-sword, as if he had been afflicted with Saint Vitus's dance. When they reached the frigate, the deck was already occupied by Tahaitians, carrying on their trading with so much eagerness and noise, that scarcely a word could be distinguished. The vessel was also surrounded by a crowd of canoes filled with all kinds of wares for barter; and so little attention was paid to the Royal Family, that it was with much difficulty our people could clear the way for their boat. Nor did the presence of these high personages attract much more notice when they had climbed the deck; their subjects continued to drive their bargains without interruption, and scarcely vouchsafed the slightest salutation. Very different would have been their conduct on the arrival of a Missionary. The Queen was probably hurt by this neglect, for she went directly into my cabin, followed by her family, and remained there till she quitted the ship. The construction of the vessel was not likely to excite her curiosity, as she was herself the owner of a well-built English merchant ship.

The goods in the cabin, however, delighted the ladies, who admired and wanted every thing; nor was it easy to convince them, that each article they coveted was indispensable to our convenience.

The officers exerted themselves to maintain the good-humour of their guests by trifling presents, and, amongst other things, gave them a piece of sham gold-lace, several yards in length, which was received with extraordinary eagerness. The Royal sisters divided it between them, and added it to the black crape trimming of their hats; and so great was the admiration excited by this novel article of finery, that the rage for gold-lace became an absolute fever among the more distinguished Tahaitian ladies.

Vain now proved the severe lessons of the Missionaries, forbidding all adornment of the person. There was no end to petitions for lace, and the more our store of it diminished, the more highly did they value the smallest piece they could obtain. The tormented husbands came every day to the ship, willingly offering a fine fat pig and eight fowls for half an ell of the false lace, to satisfy the longings of their wives. They beset me incessantly in my dwelling on shore, for this new and invaluable appendage of luxury; and were astonished beyond measure, that I, the commander, should possess none of it. The ladies who finally were unsuccessful in procuring the means of imitating a fashion thus accidentally introduced by the Royal sisters, *tout comme chez-nous*, actually fell ill and gave themselves up to the boundless lamentations of despair.

While the Royal Family remained below in the cabin, their attendants were engaged on deck in purchasing from our sailors all sorts of old clothes for a hundred times their value, in Spanish piastres. The Tahaitians have yet no notion of the value of money, which they get from the ships that touch at the island, and by their trade in cocoa-oil with New Holland.

The Missionaries have done their utmost to draw money into the country, and for this purpose have fixed prices on every article of provision, under which no one dares to sell them to foreign ships. These prices are, however, so high that nothing but necessity would induce any one to pay them, so that the ships in general rather provide themselves with old clothes, utensils of various kinds, and toys, which enable them to make most advantageous barters, and frequently even to bring away money. The plan of the Missionaries, therefore, like many other financial regulations, has been found in operation to produce a result directly contrary to the effect intended.

During the visit to my vessel, the young Princess had found an opportunity to bargain with a sailor for a sheet; having secured this treasure, she ran with it upon deck in the most extravagant joy, viewed it over and over with delight, and there formed it into a really very becoming drapery. She appeared quite conscious of her increased attractions in this attire, leaped about in the most sprightly manner, and called on all the persons of the Court to admire her. In short, a young European lady on first decorating herself with the most costly Persian shawl, would not have been half so happy as this young Princess dressed in the sailor's sheet.

At four o'clock, the dinner was served to our guests and their suite, entirely in the Russian mode; except the etiquette of placing the Royal Family a little apart from the rest of the company. The infant King had long before begun to cry from weariness, and had been carried back into the boat, where he had quietly fallen asleep. A prayer was repeated before and after dinner. The visitors seemed to think our dishes very palatable, and even the Royal Family ate with good appetite, though they had so recently made a substantial meal. Their conduct was extremely decorous, and showed much aptitude in imitation. They made use of the knives, forks, and spoons as readily as if they had been always accustomed to them; and the wine, though by no means despised, was very moderately enjoyed.

After dinner a general conversation took place, in which a man of seventy years of age distinguished himself by his animation and intelligence. He was the only individual present who had personally known Captain Cook. He asserted that he had been his particular friend, and for this reason still bore his name, which he pronounced quite correctly, although there is neither a C nor K in the Tahaitian alphabet. He boasted not a little of having accompanied Cook in his coasting voyages about the islands, and of having often slept in the same tent with him. He knew the names of all Cook's company, and could recollect the particular pursuits of each officer. To describe the manner in which Cook had observed the height of the sun, he asked for a sextant, placed himself in a stooping position, and looking fixedly upon an angle, often called with a loud voice, Stop!

He could relate the Bible-history in short extracts, from the Creation to the birth of Christ; and in order to explain the doctrine of the Trinity, he held up three fingers, pressed them together, and looked towards the Heavens. The old Cook (as he called himself,) was not entirely ignorant of geography. He said he possessed a map presented to him by his friend;— that England was an island, and much smaller than Russia; and traced out, on a map of the World being opened before him, the way by which we had come to Tahaiti.

At sunset our Royal visitants departed, highly gratified with their entertainment, and returned to the capital. This visit being over, I hoped to be at liberty to pursue my occupations in peace, but in this I was disappointed. Though my habitation was surrounded by sentinels, I was continually disturbed by swarms of curious islanders, who, troublesome as they were, were yet so gentle and good-tempered that it was impossible to be angry with them. They were particularly pleased with Dr. Eschscholz's little museum, and took pains to collect from every corner of the island, butterflies, beetles, birds, and marine productions, by way of showing their sense of the kindness with which he exhibited his treasures, often receiving from him in return some trifling present, which they considered of great value. One of them was fairly overpowered with gratitude by the gift of an old coat. With much admiration of such profuse generosity, and many expressions of rapture, he at length succeeded in cramming his large body into the garment of the infinitely smaller and more slender philosopher, and strutted about with his back hunched up, and his arms sticking out, envied by all his acquaintances for the magnificence of his attire.

Though the vice of theft has certainly greatly diminished among the Tahaitians, they cannot always refrain from endeavouring to appropriate the articles they prize so highly. For instance, I think if any one of the Tahaitian ladies had found an opportunity of stealing a bit of the mock gold lace, the temptation would have been too great to withstand. Every theft however is, on discovery, punished without distinction of persons, and the criminal, on conviction, is generally sentenced to work on the highway. A road has been made round the island, on which those who have committed great transgressions, are condemned to labour; but it is probable that neglect of prayer, or any trifling offence against the Missionaries, would also entail this punishment upon them.

We had an opportunity of observing the severity with which theft is punished. A complaisant husband could not resist the entreaties of his wife, who longed for one of our sheets. One day, when the sailors were washing in the river, he took an opportunity, unperceived as he thought, to snatch up one of these coveted articles and run off with it. Some of his countrymen, who had watched him, directly brought him back, bound him to a tree, and informed me and a Missionary of the circumstance. On reaching the spot, I already found the Judge of the district and the Missionaries Wilson and Tyrman standing beside the thief, who was still bound to the tree. Mr. Tyrman, who was especially bitter, could not refrain from abuse: he called the criminal a brute, who was not worthy to be treated as a human creature, and acted altogether as if the affair were his. This would have surprised me, as the judge of the district was present, and Mr. Tyrman had no official appointment on the island, but he was a member of the Missionary Society,—*et tout est dit.* I was now asked if I wished the offender to be whipped, as he had not the means of paying the forfeit of three pigs to the person robbed, which the law demands, in addition to the punishment of ignominious labour. I forgave him the equivalent for the pigs, and begged that he might be dismissed with a severe admonition upon the disgrace of theft, and an earnest warning for the future. This request, however, was not granted, and the unfortunate offender was taken away, still tied, to work on the highway: the Judge and Mr. Wilson concurred in assuring me that he was not a Tahaitian, but an inhabitant of another island, who had come hither with one of the tributary kings, and declared that a Tahaitian would not have stolen the sheet. The only article which we lost besides this, was an iron hoop from a barrel, and as the thief was not discovered, it remained undecided whether their assertion was well-grounded or not. At all events, it appears certain that thefts do not take place oftener than among civilized nations.

With the chastity of the Tahaitian women, the case is similar; and it does not appear to me that the breaches of this virtue are more frequent on the whole than in Europe. It was with the utmost caution and secrecy, and in the most fearful anxiety lest their errors should be betrayed to the Missionaries, that the females complied with the desires of our sailors. An accidental occurrence proved that their terrors were not groundless. A married man who possessed a house of his own, was induced to barter, according to the custom of his ancestors, the favours of his wife for some pieces of iron: he had also assisted a young man in an intrigue with a woman whose husband was not so complaisant, by lending his house as a place of rendezvous. Suddenly the owner and his wife disappeared in the night, the house was found empty next morning, and we could never learn what had become of its proprietors. Have the Missionaries already introduced the *Oubliettes?*

Having occasion one morning to visit Wilson on business, I found his door, which usually stood open, closed and fastened: I knocked several times; but the whole house seemed buried in the repose of death: at length, after loud and repeated strokes, the door was opened by Wilson, whose cheeks bedewed with tears made me apprehensive that some great calamity had befallen him; I was however soon satisfied that devotion alone had caused this emotion. In an ante-room I found four or five naked Tahaitians, of the highest rank, as Wilson told me, on their knees reading the Bible. Having apologized for what appeared to be an unseasonable intrusion, I was about to retire, but was invited by Wilson, in a friendly manner, into the inner apartment, where I found his whole family, with Messrs. Bennet and Tyrman, kneeling round a breakfast-table, on which coffee and various kinds of meat were arranged. Tyrman was praying aloud, the rest silently joining him. He thanked God for the progress the Missionaries had made in spreading Christianity. How willingly would I have concurred in his thanksgiving, had the religion they taught been true, genuine Christianity, propitious to human virtue and human happiness.

The prayer lasted yet a quarter of an hour; on its conclusion, the company rose and breakfasted with a good appetite; but offered nothing to the distinguished personages in the other apartment, who were suffered to leave the house unnoticed.

I found the bread-fruit, as baked in the ovens by the Europeans here, excellent. The natives retain their old custom of baking in the earth.

During breakfast, Wilson related the difficulties he had encountered in the conversion of the Tahaitians. They would not allow that his faith was superior to their own; and when he appealed to the miracles which confirmed the truth of the Christian doctrine, they required that he also should restore sight to the blind and raise the dead to life; the confession of his inability was met with derision, and for many years he gained no disciples. How different, in all probability, would the effect have proved, had he, instead of the miraculous history of his religion, directed the attention of the susceptible Tahaitians to its pure morality, leading so naturally to the idea of a common Father, and a fellowship of charity. O, ye Missionaries, how much blood might ye not have spared!

I received another visit from the Royal Family, accompanied this time by many of the Vice-Kings then in Tahaiti, with their consorts. Among them was the grandfather of the little monarch Pomareh the Second. After some preliminaries, my illustrious guests unanimously preferred a request in the most modest, yet pressing manner. They wished me to get a pair of boots made for the little King. His coronation, they said, would soon take place, and they did not think it decorous, on so solemn an occasion, for the Sovereign of all the Society Islands to sit barefooted on his throne.

I immediately ordered my shoemaker to provide for the Royal necessity; the measure was taken, and my complaisance rewarded by the gratitude of the whole company. At this visit, also, the guests ate and slept. I took advantage of this opportunity to observe the method of preparing the pig, always the chief dish in their feasts. A sufficiently large round hole was dug in the earth, and filled with stones. A fire was then lighted in it, and kept burning till the stones were red-hot, when the ashes and cinders were taken out, and the stones covered with large banana-leaves, upon which the pig was laid, after being thoroughly cleaned, and stuffed with the glowing stones; more leaves were spread upon it, and covered with hot stones, and finally, the hole was filled up with earth. After a certain time it was taken out, and proved a more tender and delicate roast, than the best European cook could have produced. They dress their vegetables in the same manner, and the flavour is excellent; the bread-fruit, only, I preferred as baked in Wilson's European oven.

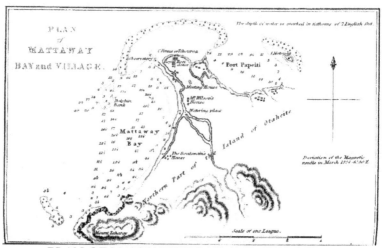

PLAN OF MATTAWAY BAY AND VILLAGE

Matarai Bay is rich in finely flavoured fish, of various, sometimes extraordinary form, and beautiful colours. The Tahaitians eat them raw, or only steeped in sea-water. Their fishing-tackle consists of nothing more than bad angling lines and hooks; to make nets as their forefathers did, would trespass too much upon the time they are obliged to spend in prayer. Hence fish is so great a rarity to them, that their eager desire for it sometimes prompts them to belie their good character, of which we had an example. One of our large nets having brought up a multitude of fine fish, the temptation was too strong to be resisted, and our friends would have forcibly shared our acquisition with us, had not our severe reproof, and the accidental appearance of the judge of the district, restrained them. They then tried to obtain the fish by barter, and offered their most valuable tools for the smallest and worst of them; I gave them, however, so many, that for once their appetite was fully satisfied with a luxurious repast.

I had heard much of an institution established by the Missionaries for the instruction of the people, and was desirous to learn what progress the Tahaitians had made in the rudiments of science. Being informed that the lessons commenced at sunrise, the first rays of that luminary found me one morning at the school-house, as I conceived the simple structure before me to be. Its walls were formed of bamboo canes, erected singly, at sufficient distances to admit the refreshing breeze from all sides, and supporting a good roof. The interior was one spacious quadrangular apartment, provided with benches, and raised seats for the teachers.

I had not waited long before the pupils of both sexes entered. They were not lively children, nor youths, whom ardour for the acquisition of knowledge led to the seat of instruction, but adults and aged persons, who crept slowly in with downcast looks, and prayer-books under their arms. When they were all assembled and seated on the benches, a Psalm was sung; a Tahaitian then rose, placed himself on an elevated bench, and read a chapter from the Bible. After this they sang again, and then knelt with their backs to the reader, who, also kneeling, repeated with closed eyes a long prayer. At its conclusion, the orator resigned his place to another Tahaitian, when the whole ceremony commenced anew; another Psalm, another chapter, and another prayer were sung and said; again and again, as I understood, a fresh performer repeated the wearisome exercise; but my patience was exhausted, and, at the second course, with depressed spirits and painful impressions, I left the assembly.

Several such meetings are established in different parts of the island, but no schools of a different character. The children are taught a little reading and writing in their parents' houses, and beyond this, knowledge is mischievous. It is true, that most of the Missionaries are incapable of communicating further instruction; but the opinion that it is easier to govern an ignorant than a well-educated community, seems here, as elsewhere, to form a fundamental principle of policy.

To pray and to obey are the only commands laid upon an oppressed people, who submissively bow to the yoke, and even suffer themselves to be driven to prayers by the cudgel!

A police-officer is especially appointed to enforce the prescribed attendance upon the church and prayer-meetings. I saw him in the exercise of his functions, armed with a bamboo-cane, driving his herd to the spiritual pasture. He seemed himself to be conscious of the burlesque attaching to his office,—at least he behaved very absurdly in it, and many a stroke fell rather in jest than in earnest. The drollery of the driver did not, however, enliven the dejected countenances of his flock.

In the prayer-house, which at first, in my simplicity, I had taken for a school, no Missionary was present. The assembly consisting, except myself, of natives only, though tolerably quiet, was not so profoundly silent as at church. I endeavoured to read in the countenances of those around me, what might be the thoughts which at the moment occupied their minds, and few were the eyes which did not, as they passed muster, speak of other matter than devotion and the Bible. Most of them appeared engaged in very profane speculations: friendly glances occasionally interchanged, betrayed the hopes of the younger devotees; while many a stately Yeri was probably considering by what means he should procure from my ship's-company an old waistcoat, or a pair of torn pantaloons in which he might appear with suitable dignity at the approaching coronation; and among the ladies, some might be weighing the pleasure of possessing a sailor's sheet, against the risks they must run to obtain it.

Exactly facing me was seated a fair one most becomingly enveloped in this envied habiliment, and enjoying with modest complacency, but visible triumph, the admiration with which the eyes of her country-women were fixed upon her garment.

I had heard from the Missionaries many wonderful accounts of the Lake Wahiria, situated among the mountains which rise in the centre of the northern peninsula. They had themselves never seen it, and considered it almost impossible for an European to reach it; even the boldest Tahaitians rarely visit it; and a saying is current in the island, that it is inhabited by an evil demon. Its depth they report to be unfathomable, and cannot conceive from what cause this huge body of water can be stationary at so great a height.

Mr. Hoffman, our mineralogist, an active young man, resolved to undertake this expedition, accompanied by three Tahaitians:—Maititi, who on our arrival had concluded a treaty of friendship with him, and adopted the name of Hoffman; Tauru, a respectable elderly man; and Teiraro, a brisk and lively young fellow. The two latter could write their own names. At first they raised many objections, assuring him that the journey, at all times difficult, was now dangerous from the waters being swollen by the rains; however, a shirt promised to each of them overcame all these obstacles, and the travellers set out at mid-day in excellent spirits. Maititi, a soldier in the royal Tahaitian army, bore the insignia of his rank in a musket, to which nothing but the lock was wanting, and a cartouche-box without powder. He had learnt a few English words, and, by their help, advised Mr. Hoffman to carry with him some presents for his countrymen: for he observed, that though hospitality and the consequence attaching to the stranger's appearance would secure him a good reception, it was desirable that a man with whom he had united himself in the bonds of friendship, should also command respect by his liberality.

They travelled on a broad fine path through forests of fruit trees, and several villages, and considered the population of this district to exceed that in the neighbourhood of Matarai. In the country of Weijoride they began to climb the mountains, and soon entered a charming valley stretching to the south-southwest, and enclosed by high steep rocks, basaltic, like those of Matarai. Down their precipitous sides clothed with the richest green rushed innumerable streamlets to swell the largest and most rapid rivulet on the island, which watered the whole extent of this luxuriant valley. Here the cocoa, palm, and the bread-fruit tree disappear, but bananas and oranges flourishing wild, produce finer and more juicy fruit than our best hot-houses.

A few scattered huts raised on the margin of the little river, gave tokens of human habitation. In one of these, occupied by an old married pair, our travellers passed the first night. Maititi seemed to consider himself quite on a foraging party, and Mr. Hoffman was under the necessity of begging him to moderate his zeal, and leave the care of the entertainment to their host. The old man fetched a pig, and Maititi, with great dexterity, played the part both of butcher and cook. Mr. Hoffman describes the operation of lighting the fire on this occasion, in the following manner:—A Tahaitian took two pieces of wood of different degrees of hardness, laid the softer upon the ground, and very rapidly rubbed its length backwards and forwards with the harder. This made a furrow, in which the dust rubbed from the wood collected, and soon became hot; it was then shaken among dry leaves and burst into a flame. The whole process seemed easy and quick; but Mr. Hoffman could not succeed in it though he made many attempts. Before supper, the master of the house recited a prayer aloud, the family repeating it after him, but not audibly. They then ate a hearty but silent meal, and prayed again before lying down to sleep. The couch offered to Mr. Hoffman was a raised platform in the hut, thickly spread with mats, with a pair of sheets of the Tahaitian manufacture, called Tapa, for its covering.

The volubility of his guides, restrained during the repast by the more important business of satisfying their appetites, now broke out to his great disturbance. They chattered almost incessantly during great part of the night with the host, whom they were probably entertaining with an account of our ship, which he had not yet visited, and of their intercourse with us. Mr. Hoffman, on taking leave in the morning, gave his host a knife, an important present, which the old man received very gratefully, as far exceeding his expectations.

The valley as they proceeded became wilder, but more beautiful: it opened to greater width, the precipices around rose to a thousand feet in height, covered from their black summits down to the valley with green shrubs of a thousand hues, through which cascades glittering like silver in the sun, rushed gurgling and foaming to the river.

At noon the travellers reached a hut inhabited by a friend of Maititi, named Tibu; the owner also of another hut some miles further up, where his wife lived with the pigs and dogs! This being the last station on the road to the Wahiria Lake, it was determined to spend the night here. Before they set forward in the morning, a large pig was tied up, to be prepared for killing on the expected return of Mr. Hoffman and his associates, whom the hospitable Tibu accompanied on the remainder of their journey.

Here every vestige of a path disappeared. At a height of seven hundred and eleven feet above the level of the sea, the travellers found enormous blocks of granite lying in a south-easterly direction. The way to Wahiria lay towards the south-south-west. They continued ascending till they reached a marsh in a rocky basin, where wild boars were running about.

Another steep precipice was to be climbed before they could reach the Valley of the Wahiria. This stretches from north to south, and forms an oval, in the centre of which lies the lake, according to barometrical measurement, one thousand four hundred and fifty feet above the level of the sea. The surrounding rocks rise perpendicularly more than two thousand feet. The lake is above a mile and a quarter in circumference, and receives the springs from the mountains. A little brook also flows into it from the north, but no channel could be found by which its waters might be carried off. The depth of the lake near the shore is eleven, and in the middle not more than seventeen toises. After Mr. Hoffman had satisfied his curiosity, he returned with his companion to Tibu's hut, and happily reached its shelter before a heavy storm that followed them had begun to discharge its fury. Exhausted by the fatigue of the march, and the oppressive heat, Mr. Hoffman threw himself on his couch to take a little repose, while his companions killed and roasted the pig. The storm now burst in tremendous violence over the hut. The thunder rolled fearfully along the valley, and reverberated from the rocks; the lightnings gave to the thick darkness a momentary illumination equal to the brightness of mid-day, and the rain pouring down in torrents, suddenly swelled the rivulet, near which the frail dwelling was erected, far above its natural channel. Whoever has witnessed a violent storm in the high mountains of a tropical country, will never lose the impression of its awfulness.

The following day being Sunday, Tauru, immediately on rising, repeated a long prayer, and then read a chapter of the New Testament, of which at least one copy was to be found in every hut. After a good breakfast, Mr. Hoffman wished to proceed, but his guides were not to be moved, and threats and entreaties were equally unavailing. They assured him that a continuation of the journey would be a profanation of the Sabbath, a crime for which they would be hanged, should it come to the knowledge of the Missionaries. This was a little too strongly expressed; and the tempting remains of the roasted pig had, no doubt, as much influence in supporting their resolution, as their religious scruples, or their fears of the Missionaries. The next morning they made no objection to setting out. Our travellers were joined on the road by many families, laden with mountain bananas, so that they arrived in a large company at Matarai.

Mr. Hoffman made several other journeys into the interior of the island, and visited Arue, the present residence of the Court. The mineralogical and geological observations made on these excursions, are reserved for a separate treatise; but some particulars concerning his intercourse with the inhabitants, may be properly introduced here.

The houses are merely built of perpendicular bamboo-canes, standing at some distance apart, to give free admission to the air. The roofs of palm-leaves are strong enough to defy the heaviest rain.

As curious after novelty as more civilized infants, the heads of the children were thrust out from every hut he passed, and the parents hospitably asked him in. When he accepted the invitation, he was always conducted to the seat of honour, a raised bench covered with matting and tapa stuff; and, after freely partaking of the best the house afforded, was considered to have paid handsomely for his entertainment with a knife. Bedsteads made of bamboo-canes, and filled with soft matting, are placed along the walls, and make very comfortable, easy couches. These pleasant little abodes, in which the greatest cleanliness is everywhere observable, are all surrounded by cultivated gardens. In the evening, they are lighted by the oily nuts of the taper-tree, fastened in rows on splinters.

Mr. Hoffman's visit to the house of his friend Maititi, excited the greatest joy. His host presented to him his wife and children, and entertained him in the most splendid manner his means would allow.

In the capital Mr. Hoffman found nothing remarkable. The palace inhabited by the Royal Family, was a spacious hut, with an ante-chamber or outer house, in which eight of the guard kept watch. Their only weapon was an old pistol fastened on a plank; this was frequently fired, probably to accustom the young King to the tumult of battle. The old King lies buried under a stone monument, in front of which three guns are kept; but, to prevent accidents, they are nailed up.

We have already mentioned the trade in cocoa-oil carried on by the Tahaitians, and the ship possessed by the Queen. This is commanded by an Englishman, and a part of the crew is also English. It was just returned from a voyage among the Society Islands, where it had been to collect tribute, and was preparing to carry a cargo of cocoa-oil, stowed in thick bamboo-canes, to Port Jackson. From the Captain, who visited me, I gained much information concerning the present state of affairs in these seas. He had learnt from ships returned from the Friendly Islands, that their King had recently conquered the Navigator Islands, which now paid tribute to him.

The map of Matarai, and of the bay which bounds it on the north-east, completed by us with the utmost care from trigonometrical surveys, is attached to this volume, and renders any further description of the coast it embraces unnecessary. In December and January, the Tahaitian summer months, the trade-wind is often interrupted by violent north-westers. Rain and storms are then frequent, and often last till April; in the other months the trade-winds blow without intermission, and the sky is always serene. For this reason, what is here called the summer, might pass for the actual winter; and as the roads of Matarai are open to the west wind, it is advisable for ships visiting Tahaiti at this season, to run into the harbour, which lies eight miles west of Venus Point. It is spacious, formed by coral reefs, protected against all winds, and has two entrances so convenient, that ships may sail either in or out with almost any wind.

The ebb and flow of the tide in the Matarai Bay differs entirely from the ordinary rules, and appears wholly uninfluenced by the moon, to which it is everywhere else subject. The rise and fall is very inconsiderable. Every noon the whole year round, at the moment the sun touches the meridian, the water is highest, and falls with the sinking sun till midnight. This phenomenon serves, as well as the sun's motion, to supply the place of clocks to the inhabitants.

According to Humboldt, the altitude of the highest mountain in Tahaiti is ten thousand feet; according to the barometrical measurement of Mr. Long, only eight thousand feet above the level of the sea.

Our first observation by chronometers, on our arrival at Matarai, gave the longitude of Venus Point as 149° 20' 30"; the true one, as given by Admiral Krusenstern on his map, is 149° 27' 20"; consequently, the error of our chronometers was 6' 50". This correction has been made in all the longitudes taken by us in the dangerous Archipelago. From our observatory on Venus Point, we found its latitude 17° 29' 17", and its longitude 149° 29'.

The variation of the needle was 6° 50' east, and its inclination 29° 30'.

The barometer ranged from 29' 80" to 29' 70"; Reaumur's thermometer from twenty-three and a half to twenty-four and a half.

The islands which I discovered on my former voyage in the ship Rurik,— the Romanzow, Spiridow, Dean's Islands, the Rurik's Chain, &c. whose longitude I had not then an opportunity to rectify upon Venus Point, lie 5' 36" more to the west than I at first supposed.

The longitude given by Captain Bellingshausen for the island which he discovered, appeared to us by 3' 10" too great.

On the morning of the 24th of March, we broke up our tent on the Venus Point, left our dwelling-house, and shipped all our instruments and effects. The afternoon was appointed for our departure. The Tahaitians now boarded the ship, bringing as many provisions as they could carry. They expressed great regret at losing us; and, to prove the disinterestedness of their good-will, would accept no presents in return. They unanimously assured us, that of all nations whose ships had visited their island, none pleased them so well as the Russians. They took leave of us with the most cordial embraces, and many of them shed tears. They accompanied us in their canoes to the mouth of the Bay, and were standing out to sea, when a sudden and violent gust of wind forced them to return. The same gust very nearly carried away one of our sails, and the proximity of the land placed us for a minute or two in a critical situation, but the coolness and skill of our officers and men relieved us from the momentary danger. In half an hour the regular trade-wind returned, and with the liveliest wishes for the future welfare of the good Tahaitians, we lost sight of their lovely island.

To the remarks concerning them already made, I will add some on their language, from the work on this subject which I have before mentioned. The author says, "The language spoken on most of the islands of the South Sea, and therefore called the Polynesian, may be considered either as primitive, or as related to, and descended from, a common source with the Malay." It is undoubtedly very old, for these people have been from an unknown period separated from all others, and before the arrival of Europeans among them, considered themselves as the whole human race.

Although, in comparison with European languages, that of Tahaiti, as belonging to an ignorant and uncultivated people, is necessarily very defective, it perhaps surpasses all others in strength, precision, and simplicity,—in the personal pronouns especially. Its resemblance to the Hebrew, in the conjugation of the verbs, as well as in the roots of some of the words, can easily be proved. Many of the words really appear of Hebrew origin: as for example, *mate*, dead; *mara*, or *maramosa*, bitter; *rapaon*, to heal, &c.

The Polynesian language being so widely extended, and spoken by the inhabitants of so many islands, who have little or no intercourse with each other, it naturally branches into many dialects. These are indeed so various, that they cannot readily be recognised as derivatives from the same stock.

The principal dialects are,—that spoken in the Sandwich Islands, or the Hawaiian; that of the Marquesas; that of New Zealand; the Tongatabuan, spoken by the inhabitants of the Friendly Islands, and the Tahaitian. All the others, as far as they are known, are more or less related to these.

The Tahaitian dialect is distinguished by its melody, as it has no broad or hissing consonants. The pronunciation is rendered difficult by its numerous diphthongs.

The substantives do not change their terminations in declension; but the cases, of which there are but three, are formed by syllables prefixed: for example—

SINGULAR.

Nom.—*Te taata*—the man.

Poss.—*No te taata*—of the man.

Object.—*He taata*—to the man—and the man.

PLURAL.

Nom.—*Te mau taata*—the men.

Poss.—*No te mau taata*—of the men.

Object.—*He mau taata*—the men—and to the men.

The Tahaitians have a great number of definite and indefinite articles, and prefixes, which they apply in a peculiar manner. The article te often stands before proper names; also before God, *Te Atua*; sometimes *o*, which then appears to be an article; as, O *Pomare*, O *Huaheine*, O *Tahaiti*. Sometimes this o is placed before the personal pronouns in the nominative case.

O *vau*, I; *o oe*, thou; *o oia*, she, he, it. In these pronouns the Tahaitian, and those languages to which it bears affinity, are particularly rich. They have not only the dual of the Orientals, but two first persons in the singular as well as plural: for example—

O *Taua*—thou and I.
O *Maua*—he and I.
O *Tatou*—you and I.
O *Motou*—we three, or several.

By this the conjugation of the verbs is made more complicated than in other languages, but it again becomes easier from neither the person nor the tense changing the word itself, but all the variations being expressed by particular particles: for instance—*motau*, to fear; *te matau nei au*, I fear; *te matau ra oau*, I feared; *i motau na oau*, I have feared; *e matau au*, I shall fear.

Since my readers will hardly wish to study the Tahaitian language very thoroughly, I here close my extracts from its grammar.—Whoever really desires to learn it must go to Tahaiti. I must, however, warn him to arm himself with patience; for though the Tahaitians are very ready with their assistance, they have quite as bad a habit as ourselves of laughing at any one who speaks their language ill,—I say this from experience.

Some months before us, the French Captain Duperré had visited Tahaiti upon a voyage of discovery, in the corvette Coquille. He returned home in safety, and is about to publish his travels, of which he has already had the goodness to send me some portions. An important acquisition to science may be expected from this work.

THE PITCAIRN ISLAND.

I DID not myself touch on this island, but I met in Chili an American Captain just returned from it, and in Tahaiti one of the earliest mothers of its population, who spoke English well enough to carry on a conversation. The information jointly obtained from both these persons, will not, I think, be unwelcome to my readers; and those who are unacquainted with the rise of this interesting colony, will perhaps find pleasure in a brief account of it.

The English government appreciating the usefulness of the bread-fruit tree, and desirous of introducing it into the West-Indian colonies, in the year 1787, commissioned the ship Bounty, under the command of Lieutenant Bligh, who had already served as master under Captain Cook, to convey a cargo of these young trees from the South Sea Islands, to the West Indies. Forty-six men formed the ship's complement.

After an excessively difficult voyage, during which he had vainly endeavoured, for thirty days, to double Cape Horn, and at length, yielding to necessity, had effected his passage by the Cape of Good Hope, he reached Tahaiti in safety in October 1788.

Although the good-natured Tahaitians seem to have given great assistance, five months were occupied in lading the vessel; perhaps because Lieutenant Bligh and his crew found their station very agreeable. During this period the crew lived in the greatest harmony with the natives, especially the women; and this may probably afford a key to the subsequent fate of Bligh.

On the fourth of April 1789, he sailed from Tahaiti, touched at one of the Friendly Islands to replace such of the young plants as had been destroyed, and on the 27th of the same month continued his course, cheered by the conviction of his ability to execute his commission, and to become the benefactor of the West Indies, by extending to them one of the greatest blessings bestowed by nature on her favourite children.

But it was otherwise written in the book of Fate. The remorseless severity with which he treated those under his command,—the insults he offered them, having subjected even his mate, Christian Fletcher, to corporal chastisement, combined with the recollection of the pleasant time spent in Tahaiti, produced a conspiracy of some of the crew, headed by Fletcher, to seize on the ship, remove from it the commander and his adherents, and, renouncing England for ever, to return to Tahaiti, and spend there the remainder of their lives in ease and enjoyment.

The conspirators kept their plan so profoundly secret, that neither Bligh nor any of those who remained faithful to him, imbibed the least suspicion of the criminal project, which was put in execution at sunrise on the 28th of April. The mate Christian, who then commanded the watch, entered, with two petty officers and a sailor, the cabin of Lieutenant Bligh, whom they found tranquilly sleeping. They fell on him, bound his hands behind his back, and threatened him with instant death if he uttered a sound, or offered the smallest resistance. Bligh, perfectly undaunted, endeavoured to grasp his weapons, and, on finding himself overpowered, called aloud for help; but the mutineers having, at the same moment, seized on all who were strangers to the plot, the unfortunate Commander had no resource but submission to his fate. He was carried on deck with no other covering than his shirt, and there found his faithful followers, nineteen in number, bound in a similar manner.

The long-boat was now lowered; Bligh, in the mean time, attempting to recall the mutineers to their duty by unavailing remonstrances, to which renewed menaces of immediate death were the only answers.

When the boat was ready, and the officers and sailors had been separately unbound and lowered into it, Christian addressed himself to Bligh: "Now, Captain, your officers and crew are ready; it is time for you to follow; any opposition will cost your life." He was then liberated, and put into the boat with his companions in misfortune, amidst the bitterest execrations for his past tyranny, from the mutineers. After some provisions had been furnished to the boat, and a compass, quadrant, and a couple of old sabres added, at the entreaty of its occupants, the mutineers set their sails and abandoned their former comrades to their fate, with shouts of "Down with Captain Bligh! Hurrah for O Tahaiti!"

A regular narrative of what afterwards befell these unfortunate outcasts would not be strictly in place here; but such of my readers as are yet unacquainted with the facts, may learn with interest, that though abandoned on the vast ocean, in an open boat only twenty-three feet long, six feet nine inches broad, and two feet nine inches deep, very scantily provisioned, and destitute of a chart, they ultimately succeeded, by unparalleled efforts, in reaching a place of safety. The boat being, at the period of its desertion, within about thirty miles of the island of Tofoa, it was determined to land there, and take in a store of provisions, then proceed to Tongatabu, and solicit permission from the King of the Friendly Islands to put their boat into a practicable condition for hazarding a voyage to India.

They effected their landing at Tofoa, and secured the boat to the strand, but were presently attacked by a multitude of savages, who saluted the defenceless strangers with showers of stones, and would soon have overpowered them, had not an heroic petty-officer, named Norton, resolved to sacrifice himself for the safety of his companions. He sprang on shore, loosened the iron chain which fastened the boat, and had only time to exclaim, Fly, fly! ere he was seized and murdered by the savages.

This melancholy occurrence discouraged the fugitives from touching at Tongatabu, or any other island inhabited by savages. All now applied to Bligh, with the unanimous entreaty that he would conduct them to some port in the possession of Europeans; and took a solemn oath of the most unconditional obedience to him in the execution of this design. In compliance with their wishes, Bligh adopted the daring resolution of passing through the Torres Straits to the island of Timor, belonging to the Dutch. The distance was about four thousand miles; it was therefore indispensable to observe the most rigid economy in distributing the provisions. The whole crew submitted, without murmuring, to the daily allowance of an ounce of biscuit, and the eighth part of a bottle of water. On the following day a storm arose, which so filled the boat with water, that the most unremitting exertions were necessary to prevent her foundering. By a second storm, accompanied with violent rain, the small remaining provision of biscuit was transformed into a sort of paste, which now constituted their only food, and even of this they were henceforward obliged to partake yet more sparingly, as the voyage proved of longer duration than was at first calculated.

Thus utterly exhausted by hunger, thirst, fatigue, wet, the burning rays of the sun, and sickness arising from such complicated sufferings, the unfortunate wanderers, after a voyage of thirty-two days, had the indescribable joy of beholding the coast of New Zealand, and entering the Torres Straits. They landed on a little uninhabited island near the coast, where they found fine flavoured fruits, oysters, and the most delicious water, all in abundance.

Refreshed by wholesome nourishment, they reposed with rapture for one night on terra firma; but the rising sun discovered new perils. The savages, armed with spears, had assembled on the opposite coast, and threatened them with a powerful irruption, which they thought it prudent to avoid, by a precipitate retreat from the island.

They sailed through the channel with fine weather, and a tranquil sea. The natives beckoned from the shore with green boughs, inviting them to land; but Bligh would not trust the intentions of this little hideous negro race.

Some other uninhabited islands served them as resting-places, and for recruiting their stores with fresh water and fruits. Reanimated by the hope of soon reaching the island of Timor and the term of their sufferings, the best spirits now prevailed among them.

But the object of their wishes was still far distant. When the boat had passed the Torres Straits, and regained the open sea, all the inconveniences and misfortunes to which they had before been subjected, returned with redoubled severity. The whole crew was sick; some were ready to expire; almost all had resigned the hope of ever again finding safety in port, and besought Heaven only for deliverance from their accumulated sufferings by a speedy death. Bligh, though himself ill, did his utmost to inspire his men with courage, assuring them that they were approaching land.

The promise did not fail. On the morning of the 12th of June, at three o'clock, the high mountains of the island of Timor rose in smiling majesty before them. This sight operated like an electric shock on the exhausted sufferers; they raised their hands to Heaven, and never certainly were thanksgivings more sincere. Two more days brought them to the Dutch settlement of Cupang, where the Governor received them with the utmost benevolence. The whole party, except one only, whose strength was entirely worn out, soon recovered their health, and found means of reaching England in March 1790.

It might have been supposed, that the terrible lesson Bligh had received would have taught him caution for the future; but it made little impression on his character. As commander of a ship of the line, his severity again provoked a mutiny; and when afterwards Governor of New South Wales, an insurrection was excited from the same excess of discipline.

To return from this digression to the history of the colonization of Pitcairn Island. The mutineers of the Bounty, after the success of their plot, unanimously elected Christian for their Captain, and sailed for Tahaiti. On their way thither, they passed the small hilly, well peopled island of Tabuai, seen in 1777 by Cook, and formed the resolution of settling there. With much difficulty they brought the ship into harbour, through numerous coral reefs. They were received in the most friendly manner by the natives, who only showed symptoms of uneasiness when they saw the new comers preparing to erect a fortress on a point of land near the harbour; even in this obnoxious undertaking, however, they assisted; but harmony was not of much longer continuance. The Europeans, confident in the superiority they derived from their weapons, soon became insolent, and especially irritated the islanders by the abduction of their women.

A sudden attack was made on Christian and his crew, who gained a height, where they defended themselves, and so effectually, that none of the party was killed, and but one man wounded; while the fire of their muskets produced great havoc among the savages. Though conquerors in this instance, they however found it advisable to quit Tabuai, and to sail once more for Tahaiti. During the voyage thither, a deep melancholy seized the mind of Christian; remorse, and dark forebodings of the future, haunted him incessantly; he shut himself up in his cabin, seldom appeared, and spoke but little.

When the Bounty again cast anchor before Tahaiti, the natives crowded to the shore, rejoicing in the speedy return of their friends, but were much surprised at missing the captain and a great part of the crew. Christian persuaded them that Captain Bligh and the other men had made a settlement on Tabuai, of which island the captain had become king, but that he himself, and those who accompanied him, preferred returning to Tahaiti, where among their kind friends, they wished to pass the remainder of their days. These innocent people gave implicit credence to his story, and heartily rejoiced in the prospect of their friends' continued residence among them. Christian's private intention, however, was to establish a colony on some unknown and uninhabited island, since it was easy to forsee, that the criminals would be first sought in Tahaiti, whenever the tidings of their proceedings should reach the English government. Being dissatisfied with some of his companions, or unable to obtain their concurrence in his views, he concerted his project with eight only of the crew, and under the strictest injunctions of secrecy. Thus arose a second conspiracy among the accomplices in guilt.

Christian and the parties to his new plot, found an opportunity of engaging the rest of the crew at a distance, while they weighed anchor and stood out to sea, with eight Tahaitians and ten women, whom they had enticed to accompany them. After a search of some weeks in those seas, they accidentally lighted upon Pitcairn Island, discovered by Carteret in the year 1767. Its extent is inconsiderable, but they found it uninhabited, and the soil fruitful, although high and rocky. Christian and his companions examined it closely, and, charmed with its luxuriant vegetation, resolved here to conceal themselves for ever from the world, hoping by this means to escape the punishment they so well merited.

All their endeavours to discover a harbour capable of admitting the Bounty, proving fruitless, they determined to place themselves under the lee of the island, save the cargo, and then destroy the ship, lest its appearance might betray them to vessels passing by.

This resolution was carried into effect, the cargo was brought quickly ashore, and the ship burnt.

At first the colony suffered from a scarcity of provisions, as the island produced neither bread-fruit nor cocoa-trees; they, however, contented themselves with a temporary subsistence on roots and fish, relying for the future improvement of their supplies on the trees destined for the West Indies, and other plants brought from Tahaiti; which had all been landed uninjured, and immediately planted. Time indeed was required before the bread-fruit and cocoa-trees would bear, but some sweet potatoes, yams, taro-roots, and others, yielded in the following year an ample harvest.

Unanimity and concord appeared firmly established among the colonists, who, by common consent, elected Christian as their head. Pretty little huts, and diligently cultivated fields of taro, yam, and potatoes, soon adorned the wilderness. After the lapse of three years, Christian became the father of a son, whom he named Friday Fletcher October Christian; but the infant's birth made its father a widower. Strongly inclined to a second marriage, and all the women being already provided with husbands, he seduced a wife from one of the Tahaitians, who, incensed at this outrage, watched an opportunity when Christian was at work on his plantation, attacked, and murdered him. Intelligence of this deed spreading quickly through the colony, produced instant retribution from the musket of an Englishman.

Long inflamed by jealousy, at the decided preference shown by their females for the strangers, the passions of the Tahaitians were exasperated beyond endurance, by this act of retaliation; they made a sudden attack by night on the English, and murdered all, except one man named Adams, who, though severely wounded, contrived to escape into the forest, and elude the pursuit of the murderers. The women rendered desperate by the massacre of their lovers, and eager for revenge, found means to obtain it the very next night. They overpowered the Tahaitians in their sleep, and murdered them to a man!

As soon as it was light in the morning, these blood-stained Megæras sought for the corpses of their beloved Englishmen, and perceiving that Adams was missing, conjectured that he might be concealed and safe; although traces of blood were visible on the ground of his hut. They accordingly searched the forest in every direction, and at last found him in a most miserable condition. They bound his wounds, carried him into a hut, and by their united care and the application of healing herbs, Adams, being young and vigorous, soon recovered his health. The affections of all the women now concentrated themselves in this one object. He became their common chief and husband, to whom they willingly promised obedience; and, according to his testimony, jealousy never embittered their lives.

Till the year 1803, consequently during fourteen years, Adams remained with his progeny concealed from the world. In this year the English Captain Falgier, sailing from Canton to Chili, landed at Pitcairn's Island, where they with astonishment encountered a people speaking English, having the most intimate knowledge of European customs, and betraying their origin in their features and complexion. Adams himself explained to him the enigma. Falgier communicated the information he had received to the English Government, but represented the situation of the island so erroneously, that it passed for a new discovery, till the English frigate Breton, in the year 1814, on her voyage from the Marquesas to the coast of Chili, also touched at the Pitcairn Island, which from the account of its discoverer Carteret, they considered uninhabited. The crew were therefore much surprised at the sight of cultivated fields, and ornamental cottages; and also of men assembled on the shore making friendly signals and inviting them to land. Some were even seen skilfully guiding their little canoes through the surf, and approaching the frigate.

The sailors were about to address them in the language of the South Sea Islands, when their surprise was not a little increased by hearing the name of the ship and her captain enquired for, in pure English. The Captain himself replied to these questions, and the conversation becoming interesting, invited his new acquaintances on board; they immediately complied, and even when the whole crew surrounded them and overwhelmed them with questions, betrayed no symptom of the timidity universal among the South Sea islanders.

The young man who had first mounted the vessel, saluted the Captain with the greatest propriety, and enquired whether he had known in England a man of the name of William Bligh. This suddenly threw a light on the mystery of the Pitcairn islanders; and they were in return asked if there was a man on the island named Christian. The answer was "No, he has been long dead, but his son is in the boat which is coming alongside." This placed the origin of the colony beyond all doubt.

The crew of the Breton were further informed, that the whole population of the island consisted of forty-eight persons—that the men were not allowed to marry before their twentieth year, and must only have one wife—that Adams had instructed them in the Christian religion—that their general language was English, but that they also understood the Tahaitian, and that they acknowledged the King of England as their sovereign. On being asked if they did not wish to go to England with the frigate, they answered "No: we are married and have children."

The sight of a ship of war and its crew, they said, was no novelty to them; and they mentioned Captain Falgier's visit to their island. A little black poodle dog which they suddenly caught sight of, put them all to flight. "That is certainly a dog," they exclaimed, as they retreated; "we have never seen one, but we know that it will bite." A little observation, however, convinced them of the animal's good-nature, and they were soon induced to play fearlessly with him. Being conducted into the cabin, they were there entertained with a breakfast, at which they behaved very modestly, and showed in their conversation much natural understanding. They said a grace before eating, and then partook with a good appetite of the provision set before them.

With much difficulty the Captain effected a landing. A pleasant path winding among groves of cocoa and bread-fruit trees, led him to a very pretty, well situated little village, whose houses, though small, were convenient and beautifully clean.

One of Adams's daughters, a young and very attractive looking girl, received the guests, and conducted them to her father, a man of sixty, but still of very vigorous appearance.

The conversation naturally fell on Christian's mutiny, in which Adams maintained he had taken no part, having been wholly unacquainted with the design till the moment of its execution. He spoke with abhorrence of the manner in which Captain Bligh and his officers and men had been treated.

The Captain proposed to Adams to accompany him back to England; but the whole colony assembling round him, with tears in their eyes, besought him not to take their good father from them. The scene affected even the Englishmen.

The Pitcairn islanders are of very pleasing exterior; they have black hair and beautiful teeth. The men are slender, and their height five feet ten inches and upwards. The dress of both sexes consists of a mantle like the Chilian pancho, and they wear hats made of reeds adorned with feathers. They still possess a great quantity of old clothes from the ship Bounty, but, with better taste than their maternal ancestors the Tahaitians, they never wear them. The island has a beautiful appearance, and is said to be extremely fruitful. Wild boars are found in the interior.

Seven years after this visit of the Breton, the American merchant-ship Eagle, whose Captain I met in Chili, touched on Pitcairn Island. He found the population already increased to a hundred persons, and was delighted with the order and good government of the little colony. Adams reigned as a patriarch king amongst them, and, as sovereign arbitrator, settled all disputes, no one presuming to object to his decision. Every family possessed a portion of land; the fields were measured off from each other, industriously cultivated, and yielding abundant crops of yams and sweet potatoes. On Sundays, the whole population assembled at Adams's house, when he read the Bible to them, exhorted them to concord and good conduct, and took pains to confirm their virtuous dispositions.

Every evening at sunset, when after the heat of the day the inhabitants of this delightful climate are revived by the refreshing coolness of the air, the young people formed a semicircle round their beloved father, while he communicated to them some knowledge of the manners and history of his native country, its connections with other nations, and the arts, inventions, and customs of the European world. Adams's knowledge is probably not very extensive, but it has sufficed to enable him to train up his numerous family in habits and information which fit them for the easy acquisition of all the arts of civilization.

His attentive auditory have accurately retained his instructions, and converse with wonderful facility on the characteristics and customs of different nations.

Abusive words are strictly prohibited; and some of the islanders, perfectly astonished at hearing a sailor on board the American vessel which visited them swear at another, enquired of the Captain whether such expressions were permitted in his country.

The Captain was enchanted with the conduct and character of this amiable people; and ascribed their virtues to the instructions and example of their patriarch. This good old man, however, expressed much anxiety concerning the future. "I cannot," said he, "live much longer,—and who shall prosecute the work I have begun? My children are not yet so firmly established, but that they are liable to fall into error. They require the guidance of an intelligent virtuous man from some civilized nation."

At Tahaiti, as already stated, I met with one of Adams's wives, who had arrived there a short time before in an European ship, and from her I learnt many of the particulars here related. She spoke tolerably good English, but with a foreign accent. This old woman had been induced, by that longing for our native home which acts so powerfully upon the human mind, to return to the land of her birth, where she intended to have closed her life, but she soon changed her mind. The Tahaitians, she assured me, were by no means so virtuous as the natives of the little Paradise to which she was now all impatience to return. She had a very high opinion of her Adams, and maintained that no man in the world was worthy of comparison with him. She still spoke with vehement indignation of the murder of the English by her countrymen, and boasted of the vengeance she had taken.

Adams, who was now very aged and feeble, had proposed to the Missionaries to send a Tahaitian as his successor; and fearing that the population of his island might exceed the means of subsistence which their quantity of arable land afforded, he was desirous of settling some of his families in Tahaiti.

With his first wish the Missionaries will certainly comply as a means of extending their dominion over Pitcairn Island also. May Adams's paternal government never be exchanged for despotism, nor his practical lessons of piety be forgotten in empty forms of prayer.

In the year 1791, the English frigate Pandora was sent, under the command of Captain Edwards, to the South Sea in pursuit of the mutineers against Bligh. Those who had remained in Tahaiti were found and carried back to England, where they were condemned to death according to the laws; the royal mercy was extended to a few only, the rest suffered the full penalty of their crime.

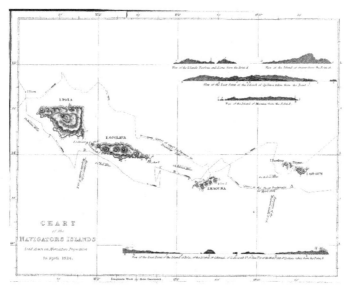

CHART OF THE NAVIGATORS' ISLANDS

THE NAVIGATORS' ISLANDS.

ON leaving Tahaiti, I proposed to pass a few days on the Radack Islands, which I had formerly discovered; and, on my way thither, determined to visit the Navigators' Islands. These are probably the same seen by Roggewin in 1721, which he called Baumann's Islands; but Bougainville has appropriated the discovery, as made by him in 1766, and given them the name they now bear, on account of the superior sailing vessels built there, and the remarkable skill the inhabitants display in their management. Neither Roggewin nor Bougainville have given their situation accurately, nor have these original errors been perfectly corrected by the unfortunate La Pérouse, or the Englishman Edwards, who alone are known to have since touched on these islands; the former visited only the more northern islands; and the latter communicated no particulars of his voyage to the public. I therefore considered it worth the trouble to complete the survey, by examining those which lay to the south of La Pérouse's track.

I at first steered past the Society Islands, lying to leeward from Tahaiti, in order to rectify their longitude; and afterwards carefully endeavoured to avoid the course taken, to my knowledge, by any former navigator.

On the 25th of March we saw, to the north, the island of Guagein, and to the north-west that of Ulietea. When the western point of the latter lay due north from us, I found its longitude, according to our chronometers, 151° 26' 30", which is nearly the same as on the maps.

The island of Maurura, on the contrary, is very inaccurately laid down; we found the longitude of the middle of this island, as we sailed past its southern coast, to be 152° 10' 40". In the evening we had already cleared the Society Islands, and were pursuing a westward course.

On the following morning we perceived a cluster of low coral islands, connected by reefs, which, as usual, enclosed an inland sea. The country was covered with thick dwarf shrubs; and, in the whole group, we saw but one cocoa-tree rising solitarily above the bushes. A multitude of sea-birds, the only inhabitants of these islands, surrounded the vessel as we drew nearer. The group stretches about three miles from North to South, and is about two miles and a half broad. Guided by observations which, from the clearness of the atmosphere, I had been enabled to make correctly immediately before they came in sight, I estimated their latitude as 15° 48' 7" South; their longitude as 154° 30'. We were the first discoverers of these Islands, and gave them the name of our meritorious navigator, Bellingshausen.

The night was stormy: morning indeed brought cheerful weather, but no cheerful feelings to our minds, for we had lost another member of our little wandering fraternity; he died, notwithstanding all the efforts of our skilful physician, of a dysentery, occasioned by the continual heat and the frequently damp air. This same year the Tahaitians suffered much from a similar disease, and died in great numbers from the want of medical assistance. The Missionaries, who only desire to govern their minds, have never yet troubled themselves to establish any institution for the health of the body.

During this and the few succeeding days, the appearance of great flocks of sea-birds frequently convinced us that we must be in the neighbourhood of unknown islands; but as from the mast-head they can only be discerned at a proximity of fifteen or sixteen miles, we did not happen to fall in with them.

On the second of April, however, we passed a little uninhabited island, something higher than the coral islands usually are. Its latitude is 14° 32' 39" South, and its longitude 168° 6'. I then considered it a new discovery, and gave it the name of my First Lieutenant, Kordinkoff; but, on my return, I learned that it had been previously discovered by Captain Freycinet, on his voyage from the Sandwich Islands to New Holland, in the year 1819; the narrative of which had not appeared when I left Europe. The situation of this island, as he has given it, corresponds exactly with my own observation.

This same night, by favour of the clear moonshine, we saw the most easterly of the Navigators' Islands, Opoun, rising from the sea like a high round mountain. Westward from it, and close to each other, lie the little islands Leoneh and Fanfueh. Near these is Maouna, with another little island at its north-east point. Forty-five miles further lies Ojalava, and ten miles and a half from it Pola, the largest, highest, and most westward of the group: connected with them are several other small islands, which I shall hereafter have occasion to mention.

As the chart which accompanies this volume accurately describes the geographical situation of all these islands, it is only necessary here to remark, that it was drawn up from the most diligent astronomical observations.

All these islands are extremely fertile, and very thickly peopled. Ojalava surpasses any that I have seen, even Tahaiti itself, in luxuriant beauty. The landscape of Pola is majestic; the whole island is one large, high, round mountain, which strikingly resembles the Mauna-roa upon the island of Owahy: it is not quite so lofty indeed as the latter, but its altitude is about the same as that of the Peak of Teneriffe.

All the islands of the South Sea are more or less formed of coral reefs, which make secure harbours; the Navigators' Islands only are not indebted to these active little animals for this advantage. We sailed round all their coasts, and could find but one open bay, which runs far inland in the island of Maouna, opposite the small island already noticed off its north-east point.

The inhabitants of these islands are still far less civilized than were the Tahaitians when first discovered by Wallis. Those of Maouna especially are perhaps the most ferocious people to be met with in the South Sea. It was they who murdered Captain de Langle, the commander of the second ship under La Pérouse, the naturalist Laman, and fourteen persons from the crews of both ships, on their venturing ashore; although they had loaded the natives with presents.

These savages attacked them with showers of stones; and the muskets of the Europeans after the first discharge, which unfortunately did but little execution, could not be reloaded speedily enough for their protection. Triumphing in their inhuman victory, they mangled and plundered the remains of their unfortunate victims.

We sailed to the scene of this dreadful occurrence, since called Massacre Bay. The appearance of the country was inviting; the shores were bordered with cocoa-trees, and the freshest vegetation enlivened the interior, but nothing betrayed that the island was inhabited; no smoke arose, and no canoe was to be seen; this was the more remarkable, as on La Pérouse's arrival, his ship, as soon as perceived by the natives, was surrounded by several hundred canoes laden with provisions. A small canoe, carrying only three men, at length rowed towards us; we laid to, and by signs gave permission to the savages to come on board; this they could not resolve upon; but one of them climbed the ship's side high enough to see over the deck, and handed to us a few cocoa-nuts, all the provisions they had brought; a piece of iron, which we gave him in return, he pressed to his forehead in sign of thankfulness, and then bowed his head. He examined the deck a long time with prying and suspicious glances, without speaking a word; then suddenly commenced a long pathetic harangue, growing more and more animated as he proceeded, and pointing with passionate gestures, alternately to the ship and the land. His eloquence was quite thrown away on us; but the silence with which we listened, might probably lead him to suppose that we attached some importance to it. His confidence gradually increased, and he would perhaps have spoken longer, had not his attention been arrested by the approach of several canoes.

We were soon surrounded by the descendants of the barbarian murderers; perhaps some of the actors in the atrocious deed might even themselves be amongst the crowd which now assembled around us. This wild troop appeared timid at first, but our orator having encouraged them, they became so impudent and daring, that they seemed disposed to storm the ship. I ranged my sailors fully armed round the deck, to keep off such disagreeable visitants, but with strict orders to avoid hurting them. It was, however, only the bayonets and lances which prevented the multitude from climbing into the ship; and some of the most daring, by patiently enduring heavy and repeated blows, even succeeded in reaching the deck; they grasped with both hands any object they could cling to, so pertinaceously, that it required the united efforts of several of our strongest sailors to throw them overboard. Except a few cocoa-nuts, they brought us no kind of provisions, but by pantomimic gestures invited us to land; endeavouring to signify that we should be richly provided on shore with every thing we wanted. The savages had probably destined for us the fate of De Langle and his companions; they appeared unarmed, but had artfully concealed clubs and short lances in their canoes.

A very few of them, whom we permitted to remain on deck, behaved as impudently as if they had been masters of the ship; they snatched from my hands some little presents I was about to distribute among them, exhibiting them to their companions in the canoes below. This excited amongst the latter a terrific rage, and, with noise and gestures resembling madness, they endeavoured to frighten us into compliance with their desire to come on board. Only one among them received the presents we made him, with any appearance of modesty or thankfulness; the others seemed to consider them as a tribute due to them. This more decorous personage bowed towards me in almost an European fashion, pressed the articles given him several times to his forehead, and then, turning to me, rubbed the point of his nose pretty roughly against mine. This young savage was probably a person of rank, who had received a particularly good education; he was of a cheerful temper, examined every thing very closely, and made many remarks to those in the canoes, which were apparently considered extremely witty, for he was always answered by bursts of laughter. The rest of his countrymen who remained on board, became very troublesome; like the beasts of the deserts, scarcely more wild than themselves, they tried to seize by main force whatever we would not willingly give them. One of them was so tempted by the accidental display of a sailor's bare arm, that he could not help expressing his horrible appetite for human flesh;—he snapt at it with his teeth, giving us to understand by unequivocal signs, that such food would be very palatable to him. This proof that we were in communication with cannibals, needed not the picture presently conjured up by our imagination, of the detestable meal which the unfortunate Frenchmen had doubtlessly afforded to their murderers, to complete our disgust and aversion, and to accelerate the expulsion of the remaining savages from our vessel.

The inhabitants of many of the South Sea islands are still cannibals, and most of them, even where this abominable propensity does not prevail, are of so artful and treacherous a character, that none should venture among them without the greatest precaution. Their friendliness arises from fear, and soon vanishes when they think themselves the strongest, and are not exposed to vengeance. I would not even advise placing too much confidence in the inhabitants of Radack, who are certainly among the best of these islanders. It is only when ideas of right and wrong are steadily fixed, that man becomes really rational; before this, he is like other animals, the mere slave of his instincts.

The inhabitants of Maouna are probably the worst of these tribes; those we saw were at least five feet and a half in height, slender, their limbs of a moderate size, and strikingly muscular; I should have thought their faces handsome, had they not been disfigured by an expression of wildness and cruelty; their colour is dark brown; some let their long, straight, black hair hang down unornamented over neck, face, and shoulders; others wore it bound up, or frizzed and crisped by burning, and entangled like a cap round the head: these caps are coloured yellow, and make a striking contrast with the heads which remain black. Some, again, coloured their hair red, and curled it over their shoulders like a full-bottomed wig. A great deal of time must be required for this mode of dressing, a proof that vanity may exist even among cannibals. The glass beads they obtained from us they immediately hung over their neck and ears, but had previously no ornaments on either. Most of them were quite naked; only a few had aprons made of the leaves of some kind of palm unknown to us, which from their various colours and red points resemble feathers. Since the time of La Pérouse, the fashion in tattooing appears to have very much altered: he found the inhabitants of the South Sea Islands so tattooed over the whole body, as to have the appearance of being clothed;—now most of them are not tattooed at all; and those few who are, not with various drawings as formerly, but merely stained blue from the hip to the knee, as though they had on short breeches.

In the canoes we saw a few women who were all very ugly: these disagreeable creatures gave us to understand that we should by no means find them cruel—a complaisance which did not render them the less disgusting. La Pérouse here describes some attractive females: these were as brown as the men, and as little dressed; their hair was cut short off, with the exception of two bunches stained red, which hung over their faces.

Scarcely one of these savages was without some remarkable scar: one of them attracted our attention by a deep cut across the belly. We contrived to ask him how he got this cicatrice; and he pointed to his lance, from which it may be inferred that they are not unaccustomed to war, either with their neighbours or each other, and that they are possessed of skilful surgeons. No one of this people seemed to exercise any authority over the others. Either no chief accompanied the party who came to us, or the term does not signify much power or distinction.

The few fruits which they brought with them were exchanged for pieces of iron, old barrel-hoops, and glass beads; on the latter especially they set great value, and even brought forward some of their concealed arms, and offered them in exchange for this costly decoration. Meanwhile the crowd of canoes round the ship grew more and more numerous, and in the same proportion the boldness of the savages increased. Many of them rose up in their canoes, and made long speeches to, or at us, accompanied by angry and menacing gestures, which drew shouts of laughter from their companions. At length the screaming and threatening with clubs and doubled fists became general. They began to make formal preparations for an attack, and we again had recourse to bayonets and lances to keep them at a distance. I confess that, at this moment, I had need of some self-command to overcome my inclination to revenge on the ferocious rabble the fate of La Pérouse's companions.

Our guns and muskets were all ready loaded. A sign from me would have spread dismay and death around us; and had we stayed longer among this brutal race, we must inevitably have made them feel the power of our cannon.

We therefore spread our sails, and the ship running swiftly before the wind, many of the canoes which had fastened themselves about her were suddenly upset. Those who fell into the water took their ducking very coolly, righted their canoes again, and threatened revenge on us with the most violent gestures. Several of them clung like cats to the sides of the ship, with nails which might have rivalled those of a Chinese Mandarin; and we had recourse to long poles as the only means of freeing ourselves from such undesirable appendages.

At the western promontory of the island we again lay to, and purchased two pigs from some canoes which soon came up. The savages here in no other respect differed from those of Massacre Bay, than by conducting themselves in a rather more peaceable manner, probably from fear, as their number was small.

In the evening the island of Olajava appeared in sight; and about seven miles from a little island lying in its neighbourhood, several canoes, carrying two or three men each, rowed towards us, deterred neither by the distance nor the increasing darkness. Our visitors proved to be merry fishermen, for their carefully constructed little canoes adorned with inlaid muscle-shells, were amply provided with large angling hooks made of mother-of-pearl, attached to long fine lines, and various kinds of implements for fishing, and contained an abundance of fine live fish of the mackerel kind.

An expression of openness and confidence sat on the countenances of this people. Our purchases were carried on with much gaiety and laughter on both sides. They gave us their fish, waited quietly for what we gave them in return, and were perfectly satisfied with their barter.

Their attention was strongly attracted to the ship. They examined her closely from the hold to the mast-head, and made many animated remarks to each other on what they saw. If they observed any manœuvres with the sails or tackle, they pointed with their fingers towards the spot, and appeared to watch with the most eager curiosity the effect produced.

It was evident that this people, sailors by birth, took a lively interest in whatever related to navigation. Their modest behaviour contrasted so strikingly with the impudent importunity of the inhabitants of Maouna, that we should have been inclined to consider them of a different race, but for their exact resemblance in every other particular, even in the dressing of their hair, though this was even more elaborately performed—an attention to appearance which is curious enough, when compared with the dirty, uncombed locks of European fishermen; but among the South Sea Islanders fishing is no miserable drudgery of the lowest classes, but the pride and pleasure of the most distinguished, as hunting is with us. Tameamea, the mighty King of the Sandwich Islands, was a very clever fisherman, and as great an enthusiast in the sport as any of our European princes in the stag chase. As soon as the increasing darkness veiled the land from our sight, our visitors departed, and we could hear their regular measured song long after they were lost from view.

The little island they inhabit not being marked on any map, it is probably a new discovery. By what name the natives called it I could not learn; and therefore, to distinguish it from three other small islands lying to the north, mentioned by La Pérouse, I gave it the name of Fisher's Island. It rises almost perpendicularly from the sea to a considerable height, and is overgrown with thick wood.

On the following day we sailed with a brisk wind to the island of Olajava, for the purpose of surveying the coast. A number of canoes put off from the land, but could not overtake the ship; and I would not lie to, on account of the hinderance it occasioned to our work. In the afternoon we found ourselves near the little island lying off the north-west point of

Olajava, called by La Pérouse the Flat Island. A hill situated in its centre has, in fact, a flat surface, which La Pérouse, at a distance of thirty miles, mistook for the whole island, because the low land which surrounds it was not within the compass of his horizon.

For the same reason he could not observe that the eastern part of this island is connected with the western coast of Olajava by two reefs forming a basin, in the middle of which is a small rock. If these be indeed coral reefs, which they certainly resemble, they are the only ones I have remarked in the Navigators' Islands.

The Flat Island, which, for the reason above mentioned, occupies a much larger space on our map than on that of La Pérouse, is entirely overgrown with wood, and has a very pleasant appearance. At a little distance from this, to the north-west, another little island, which does not appear to have been observed by that Voyager, rises perpendicularly from the sea. Its sloping back is crested with a row of cocoa-trees so regularly arranged, that it is difficult to conceive them planted by the unassisted hand of Nature; viewed laterally from a short distance, they present the form of a cock's-comb, on which account I gave the island this name, to distinguish it from the rest. On its western side a high conical rock is covered from top to bottom with a variety of plants, evincing the prolific powers of Nature in these regions, where vegetation is thus luxuriantly fastened on the most unfavourable soils.

North-west of this rock lies a third small island, exceeding both the others in elevation: its sides fall precipitously to the sea, and the upper surface describes a horizontal line thickly clothed with beautiful trees. As its circumference is only three miles and a half, it can hardly be the same that La Pérouse has called Calinasseh. Probably he did not observe this island at all, but took the high round mountain on the low north-east point of Pola for a separate island, to which he gave the name of Calinasseh. The promontory of Pola deceived us also at a little distance, but a closer examination convinced us of our error, and I transferred the name of Calinasseh to the above-mentioned small island.

When the Flat Island lay about three miles to our right, the wind again died away. This opportunity was not lost by the natives of Olajava, who had all the while followed us in their canoes. They exerted themselves to the utmost, and their well worked little vessels swiftly skimmed the smooth surface of the sea to the accompaniment of measured cadences, till they at last reached the ship.

A horde of canoes now put off towards us from the Flat Island, and we were soon surrounded by immense numbers of them, locked so closely together, that they seemed to form a bridge of boats, serving for a market well stocked with fruits and pigs, and swarming with human beings as thick as ants on an anthill: they were all in high spirits, and with many jests extolled the goods they brought, making much more noise than all the traffic of the London Exchange. Even on our own deck we could only make ourselves heard by screaming in each other's ears.

Our bartering trade proceeded, however, to our mutual satisfaction. Those who were too far off to reach us endeavoured by all sorts of gesticulation, and leaping into the air, to attract our notice. Many of the canoes were in this manner upset,—an accident of little consequence to such expert swimmers, and which only excited the merriment of their companions.

Accident gave us specimens of their extraordinary skill in diving. We threw some pieces of barrel-hoops into the sea, when numbers of the islanders instantly precipitated themselves to the bottom, and snatched up the booty, for the possession of which we could plainly distinguish them wrestling with each other under the water. They willingly obeyed our orders not to come on deck, and fastened their goods to a rope, by which they were drawn on board, waiting with confidence for what we should give them, and appearing content with it. Some few had brought arms with them, but for trading, not warlike purposes; and although so vastly superior to us in numbers, they behaved with great modesty. We saw no scars upon them, like those of their neighbours of Maouna—a favourable sign, though they certainly seemed to belong to the same race. It would be interesting to know the cause of this striking difference.

In less than an hour we had obtained upwards of sixty large pigs, and a superfluity of fowls, vegetables, and fruits of various kinds, covering our whole deck, all of which cost us only some pieces of old iron, some strings of glass beads, and about a dozen nails. The blue beads seemed to be in highest estimation. A great fat pig was thought sufficiently paid for by two strings of them; and when they became scarce with us, the savages were glad to give two pigs for one such necklace.

Some of the fruits and roots they brought were unknown to us; and their great size proved the strength of the soil. The bananas were of seven or eight species, of which I had hitherto seen but three in the most fruitful countries. Some of them were extremely large, and of a most excellent flavour. One of the fruits resembled an egg in size and figure; its colour was a bright crimson; and on the following day when we celebrated the Easter festival after the Russian fashion, they supplied to us the place of the Easter eggs.

I must yet mention two more articles of our marketing—namely, tame pigeons and parrots. The former are widely different from those of Europe both in shape and in the splendour of their plumage; their claws are also differently formed. The parrots are not larger than a sparrow, of a lively green and red, with red tails more than four times the length of their whole bodies. All these birds, of which great numbers were brought to us, were so tame, that they would sit quietly on the hand of their master, and receive their food from his mouth; the inclination for taming them, and the method of treatment, is favourable evidence of the mildness which characterises this people.

How many other unknown plants and animals may exist among these islands, where Nature is so profuse! and how much is it to be regretted that no secure anchorage can be found, which would enable an European expedition to effect a landing with proper precautions. Some idea may be formed of the dense population of the Flat Island, from the fact that, small as is its extent, above sixty canoes, each containing seven or eight men, came to us from it in less than an hour; and had we stayed longer, the canoes must have amounted to some hundreds, as the whole sea between us and the island was rapidly covering with increasing numbers.

Our market became still more animated when, the ship's provision being completed, I gave permission to the sailors to trade each for himself; as hitherto, to avoid confusion, the bargains had all been made by one person. Now some wanted one thing, some another from the canoes; and buttons, old bits of cloth, and pieces of glass, were offered in exchange. The noise became louder and louder; and the sailors laid in such a stock of their own, that for weeks afterwards their breakfast-table was always provided with a roasted pig stuffed with bananas, and their palates gratified with abundance of delicious fruits. They unanimously declared that they had never seen so rich a country.

Our trade was interrupted by the appearance of a great canoe surrounded with lesser ones, which, advancing towards us, drew the attention of all the natives. They called out *Eige-ea Eige*, and hastened to give place to the new-comers. The canoe, rowed by ten men, large and elegantly embellished with muscle-shells, soon approached us. The heads of the rowers and of the steersman were decorated with green boughs, probably in token of peace.

In the fore part of the vessel, on a platform covered with matting, sat an elderly man cross-legged in the Asiatic fashion, holding a green, silk European parasol, which we conjectured must have belonged to one of the unfortunate companions of La Pérouse, and have been obtained by this chief from Maouna. His clothing consisted of a very finely plaited grass-mat, hanging like a mantle from his shoulders, and a girdle round his waist.

His head was enveloped in a piece of white stuff, in the manner of a turban. He spoke a few words, accompanied by a motion of the hand, to his countrymen or subjects, who immediately made way for his canoe to come alongside; and on our invitation he came on board attended by three persons.

He was not tattooed, was about six feet high, thin, but vigorous and muscular. His features were not handsome but agreeable; his countenance was intelligent and reflective; his behaviour modest and decorous.

On entering the ship, he inquired for the *Eigeh*, and I was pointed out to him; he approached me, bowed his head a little, spoke a few words which I did not understand, and then took hold of my elbows with both hands, raised them up several times, and repeated the English words "Very good." After this welcome, which I returned in an European manner, he gave me to understand that he was Eigeh of the Flat Island, and commanded his attendants to lay at my feet the presents he had brought for me, consisting of three fine fat pigs, which he called *boaka*, and some fruits. I presented him in return with a large hatchet, two strings of blue beads, and a coloured silk handkerchief, which I bound for him myself over his turban. The *Eigeh* appeared excessively happy in the possession of these treasures, and tried to express his thankfulness by various gesticulations, and the repetition of the words "Very good." He also seemed to hold the blue beads in great estimation, and could not feel convinced that all those riches actually belonged to him. He inquired in pantomime if he might really keep both necklaces; and on my assuring him that he might, the old man forgot his dignity, and jumped about like a boy with the beads in his hand, calling out, "Very good! very good!" A fat treasurer shared the joy of his lord, and punctiliously imitated its expression, though not without some difficulty. When this tumult of pleasure had a little subsided, the latter produced a small basket very prettily plaited, and provided with a lid, and placed in it the costly acquisitions of the *Eigeh*; who himself took from it a Spanish dollar, and endeavoured to make me comprehend the question, whether this would purchase more blue beads.

To judge if he had any idea of the value of money, I offered him a single bead for his dollar; he immediately closed with the bargain, and, fearing that I might repent of mine, snatched up the bead and thrust the money into my hand. I returned it to him; but, to his delight and astonishment, left him in possession of the bead. I now tried to learn from him how he came by this coin. He soon comprehended my meaning, pointed to the south, named Tongatabu, one of the Friendly Islands, which are some days' voyage from his own, and gave us to understand that he had sailed thither in his own vessel, and had there met with a ship from whose *Eigeh* he had obtained the dollar as well as the parasol. The boldness and skill these islanders display in the management of their fragile canoes, guiding them on long voyages merely by the sun and stars, in a region where the trade-wind is seldom constant, is most surprising.

I also made some little presents to the suite of the *Eigeh*, and the good people were lost in amazement at their costliness, till their attention was withdrawn from them to the ship itself. Their inquisitive eyes wandered in all directions, and their astonishment and admiration was loudly expressed. The *Eigeh* contemplated the objects before him with more tranquillity, and asked but few questions, having already seen a ship, which his companions probably had not.

He remarked, however, with wonder the number of our guns and muskets, which he called *Puas*; counted them several times over, and clasped his hands above his head to express his surprise. He intimated to us that he knew the effect they produced, by pointing to a gun, trying to imitate the sound of the report, and then closing his eyes and hanging his head. He explained this to his companions, who were so terrified by what he told them, that they would not again venture near the guns.

Meanwhile our traffic was renewed, though rather confusedly, from the impatience of the islanders to dispose of their property; the *Eigeh* grew angry at this, and pressed me much to fire my *puas* on the boisterous mob. Was he then really acquainted with their destructive power, and so indifferent about human life? Or, was he aware of the possibility of firing with blank cartridges? This remained uncertain.

A telescope which I held in my hand attracted the observation of the chief, who took it for a gun. I directed him to look through it; but the sudden vision of the distant prospect brought so close to his eye that he could even distinguish the people on the strand, so terrified him, that nothing could induce him to touch the magic instrument again.

He took much pains to persuade me to visit him on shore, embraced me repeatedly, and gave me to understand that we might cast anchor by his island, and that we should there have as many pigs as we pleased. At length he took my arm, and leading me to the railing, whence we could see the throngs of islanders busied with their barter, pointed to the women among them, whom he called *waraki*, shook his head, and said "No very good." Then he pointed to the island, and said in a kind tone, "Very good *waraki*." I very easily withstood this last temptation, strong as the *Eigeh* seemed to think it; but I would willingly have seen the beautiful country, had it been possible to make a landing under the protection of our guns, for which however the wind was not favourable: a longer stay might besides have rendered our situation critical. We had a perfect calm, and were driven by a strong current towards the land; I therefore took advantage of the first puff of wind to make as much sail as I could, amidst the loud lamentations of the islanders, who expressed their regret in a mournful parting song.

The *Eigeh*, perceiving that his invitations would not be accepted, took a friendly leave of us: he seized me again by my elbows, hung his head, repeated several times the word "*Marua*," and departed. The canoes did not follow him, but remained near us, as our vessel could make but little way on account of the slackness of the wind.

The traffic was now over, and the attention of our companions therefore free to observe all our proceedings in the ship. Some of them thought to amuse us by making leaps into the air, and then begged for a reward. We did not disappoint them, and the tricks were reiterated, till a sudden gust of wind changed their merriment into consternation. The canoes immediately ahead of the ship could not leave its passage clear in time to prevent our running down great numbers of them. In a moment our majestic vessel had distanced the multitude of its diminutive attendants, leaving extreme confusion behind it. The islanders' skill in navigation, however, enabled them speedily to recover from the shock, and the wind falling again, they succeeded in overtaking us. In the effort to accomplish this, they left all those to their fate who were still swimming about in search of their lost oars, and took no notice whatever of their cries for assistance. We pointed their attention to their forsaken companions, but the volatile creatures only laughed, and not a single canoe would return to take them in. At length, towards nightfall, they left us with the cry of "*Marua! Marua!*"

Among these islanders we observed the disease of elephantism, from which the Tahaitians suffer so much; otherwise they appeared healthy. If, as the Tahaitian captain said, they are subject to the Friendly Islanders, and must pay a yearly tribute to Tongatabu, the island Maouna, which Nature herself has made a strong fortress, and whose inhabitants are such fierce warriors, is probably excepted.

The following day we surveyed the magnificent island of Pola. Its lofty mountain was enveloped in thick white clouds, which seemed to roll down its sides, while the majestic summit rose into a cloudless region above them. The most luxuriant vegetation covers even its highest points. From a considerable elevation down the sea-shore, the island presents a charming amphitheatre of villages and plantations, and confirmed us in the opinion, that the Navigators' Islands are the most beautiful in the Southern Ocean, and consequently in the whole world.

The shore was thronged with people, some of whom pushed their canoes into the sea to approach us, and others stood quietly watching us as we sailed past. The recurrence of a calm enabled the islanders to reach us, and our traffic with them was carried on in the same manner as with the natives of the Flat Island.

To avoid repetition, I shall only remark, that they seemed more shy than our yesterday's friends; that one of them offered us a red paint for sale; and that another cheated us. The former daubed his face with some of the colour to show us its use. Since none of them were painted with it, it is probably only used in war, or on grand occasions. The cheat remained, when the darkness had driven the other islanders homewards, bargaining with us for the price of a hog: a sack was lowered to him with the required payment, and when drawn up was found to contain a dog. The rascal had made off, but we sent a bullet after him, which seemed to produce no small dismay.

On the following day, the 7th of April, having completed our observations, we took our course with a fresh trade-wind and full sails towards the north-west, in a direction where, according to the opinion of hydrographers, islands must lie.

With respect to our geographical observations on the Navigators' Islands, I must make one remark—that all the longitudes found by us differ from those of La Pérouse by from 20 to 23', and the points observed lying so many miles more easterly than he considered them. His observations were grounded on the distance of the moon, which always gives a false longitude unless there is an opportunity of seeing the moon at equal distances, right and left, from the sun. Our longitudes were fixed by good chronometers, which having been regulated at Cape Venus, could not in so short a time have made any important error.

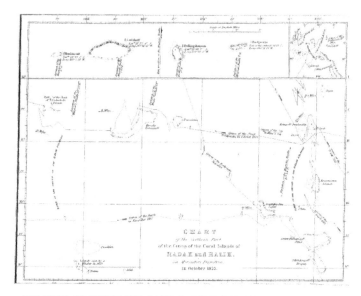

CHART OF THE ISLANDS OF RADAK AND RALIK

RADACK CHAIN OF ISLANDS.

ON the 8th of April, at noon, we found ourselves, according to our observation, in the latitude 11° 24' South, and in the longitude 174° 24'. We had left the north-west point of the island of Pola one hundred and forty miles behind us: the weather was fine, the horizon very clear, but we looked in vain from the mast-head for land.

Hence we gave up any further search in this quarter, and directed our course to the north, for the shortest way to cut the Equator, and then, by the help of the north-east trade-wind, to reach Radack, where we intended to stop and make observations on the pendulum, the results of which, in the neighbourhood of the Equator, would be important to us. I appointed Otdia, belonging to this chain of islands, for our residence, as affording the most convenient anchorage for large ships.

We were so much delayed by calms, that we could not till the 19th of April reach the ninth degree of south latitude. Here we encountered gusts of wind and torrents of rain, and a current carried us daily from twenty to thirty miles westward. When we were under three degrees south latitude, and one hundred and eighty degrees longitude, the current suddenly changed, and we were driven just as strongly to the East,—a circumstance too remarkable to be passed over in silence. At a distance from land in the vicinity of the Equator, the currents are always westerly. Here it was precisely contrary; from what cause I am unable to explain.

From the fifth degree of south latitude to the Equator, we daily perceived signs of the neighbourhood of land. When we were exactly in 4° 15' latitude, and 178° longitude, heavy gales brought swarms of butterflies and small land-birds to the ship; we must therefore have been near land, but we looked for it in vain; and this discovery remains for some future navigator.

On the 22nd we cut the Equator in the longitude 179° 43', and once more found ourselves in our own Northern hemisphere—nearer to our native country, though the course by which we must reach it would be still longer than that we had traversed. Our old acquaintance the Great Bear showed himself once more, and we looked upon him with joy, as though he had brought intelligence from our distant homes.

We now again employed Parrot's machine to draw up water from a depth of 800 fathoms. Its temperature was only six degrees of Reaumur, while that of the water at the surface was twenty-three degrees.

A tolerably strong wind, which blew during several successive days, brought us within sight of the Radack Islands, on the morning of the 28th of April.

To those who are yet unacquainted with these islands, and cannot or will not have recourse to my former voyage, I must be excused giving a few particulars concerning them.

In the year 1816, in the ship Rurik, I discovered the chain of islands called by their inhabitants, Radack. It consists of several groups lying near each other, and these again of many small islands united by reefs and surrounding great basins of water. All these being formed by the coral insect, are very low, and still but thinly covered with soil, so that they want the luxuriance of vegetation usual in this climate; their population is scanty; and the most important island of a group commonly gives its name to the whole.

The Radackers are tall and well made, of a dark brown complexion; their black hair is neatly bound up, and that of the women decorated with flowers and strings of muscle-shells. Their features are soft and agreeable, and many of both sexes may be considered beautiful. They attain a great age, and though less robust than some other South Sea islanders, and subsisting wholly on fish and vegetables, are generally healthy. In gentleness and good-nature they excel them all, even perhaps the Tahaitians.

The chief or sovereign of all these islands is named Lamari: the chiefs of the particular groups are subordinate to him; and under these are the chiefs of the separate islands composing each group. The chief of the group Otdia is called Rarik. I gave his portrait in my former voyage, and was particularly pleased with him, and with another native of the same group, named Lagediak. An inhabitant named Kadu of the group Kawan, no native, but thrown there by a storm from the island of Ulle, made the voyage from Otdia to Unalaschka and back with us in the ship Rurik, and gained the good-will of the whole crew. He gave us some instructions in the Radack language; and on our second visit could interpret pretty well between us and the islanders, as he already spoke a little Russian: his portrait also is prefixed to one of the volumes of my former voyage.

After an absence of eight years, I was now again in sight of my favourite Radack Islands, where I had passed several weeks among some of the best of Nature's children. Whoever has read my former narrative, will imagine the pleasure with which I anticipated my certain welcome; I pictured to myself a meeting on which the heavens themselves appeared to smile. It was an uncommonly fine day, and a fresh and favourable wind carried us quickly towards land. Our inquiring glances soon showed us from the deck, on the island Otdia, the airy groves of palms which enclose the residence of Rarik, and under whose shade I had so often sat among the friendly islanders. We could now distinguish boats sailing about on the inner basins, from one island to another, and a crowd of people running to the shore to gaze at the ship. I knew my timid friends too well, not to guess what was passing in their minds. I had indeed, on parting from them, promised to visit them again, but the length of time which had since elapsed had probably extinguished this hope; and they would easily perceive that the great three-masted ship they now saw was not the small two-masted Rurik of their acquaintance. If, therefore, the first glimpse of the vessel had flattered them with the expectation of seeing me again, their pleasure had been ere this converted into fear. Uncertain how they might be treated by the strangers, the women and children fled to the interior, and all the canoes were set in motion to carry their little possessions to some place of comparative safety. The most courageous among them advanced armed with spears to the shore, displaying their valour while the danger was yet distant.

It is not surprising that timorous apprehensions should agitate these poor people on the appearance of a strange vessel. Their western neighbours, the inhabitants of the island of Ralick, and of the southern islands of the groups Mediuro and Arno, which are much more thickly peopled, sometimes attack them with a superior force, plunder them, destroy their fruit-trees, and leave them scarcely subsistence enough to preserve them from starving. They had indeed imbibed from the crew of the Rurik a favourable opinion of white people; but the ship which now approached them was a monster in comparison of it, and they were excusable in supposing it manned by another and unknown race.

We now reached the group Otdia, and sailed close under the outward reef, towards the Schischmaref Strait, through which I proposed to enter the basin. The sight of the ship diffused terror throughout all the islands as we passed, and the natives fled for concealment to the forests. As we approached the Lagediak Strait, the breeze was sufficient to warrant us in venturing through it; I therefore gave up my intention of entering by the Schischmaref Strait where the wind would be against us, spread all sail, and soon rode on the placid waters of the basin. I would not however advise seamen, without an adequate inducement, to choose this strait: it is so narrow, that stones might easily be thrown across from either shore; while, on the contrary, the breadth of the Schischmaref Strait admits of tacking, and renders its passage easy with a good ship. The water in the Lagediak is so transparent, that in a depth of fourteen fathoms, every stone at the bottom is discernible; the officer who sat in the tops on the watch for shallows, deceived by this appearance, expected every moment that the ship would run aground.

We continued to sail pleasantly on the beautiful smooth water of the basin, but the wind blowing directly off the island of Otdia, (after which the whole group is named, and where I hoped to meet with Rarik,) I was compelled, as it grew dark, to cast anchor before the island of Ormed, in a depth of thirty-two fathoms, on a bottom of fine coral sand. Till the ship entered this natural harbour, the courage of the islanders did not quite forsake them, as they supposed the entrance to be unknown to us, and the exterior coast they trusted to the protection of the surf; but when we had penetrated into the basin, the panic became universal. We observed a constant running backwards and forwards on the shore; canoes hastily laden and rowed away, some to the right and some to the left, but none coming near us. The whole island of Ormed seemed, on our arrival, to have fairly given up the ghost. It was not till after dark that we could perceive any trace of life upon it; large fires were then kindled in two places at some distance from each other, while many smaller ones were flickering between them. We could also hear a sort of shrieking song, accompanied by the drum, which I knew to be their manner of calling on the gods for help, and which proved the extent of the alarm we had occasioned. This religious rite lasted through the night, but with the morning's dawn my friends had again disappeared, and the stillness of death prevailed as before.

We weighed anchor, and endeavoured by tacking to reach Otdia; and in so doing, often came very close upon the little picturesque bright green islands which studded the sparkling lake. The fresh morning breeze wafted aromatic odours towards us; but the huts of the inhabitants stood empty and desolate. When we were near Otdia, we again descried canoes sailing as close as possible to the shore. The population was busy on the strand, but no one seemed rightly to know what should be done in this alarming crisis. We next saw a long procession of islanders, bearing branches of palm as symbols of peace, taking advantage of the ebb-tide to cross the reef towards Otdia, and carrying baskets of cocoa-nuts and other fruits on poles. Hence it appeared that my friends had yielded to their destiny, and hoped to win the favour of the intruders by humility and presents. From their former dismay, I anticipated that Kadu was absent, or he would have inspired his countrymen with more confidence.

We dropped anchor at noon opposite Otdia, on the same spot where the Rurik formerly rode. I then ordered a small two-oared boat to be lowered, and to make my first visit as little formidable as possible to my friends, went ashore with only Dr. Eschscholz and two sailors. We rowed direct to Rarik's residence, where no human being was visible. A little canoe, bringing three men from a neighbouring island, now neared the shore, but immediately endeavoured to escape on observing that we steered towards it; in vain I waved a white handkerchief, a signal I had formerly been accustomed to make; they persisted in crowding sail, and taking all possible pains to get out of our reach; but their extreme anxiety now rendered that difficult which they usually perform with great dexterity. While they disputed vehemently among themselves, we gained materially upon them, and their entangled ropes refusing the assistance of their sails, they were on the point of trusting to their skill in swimming for safety, when two words from me changed all this terror into equally clamorous joy. I called to them "*Totabu*," the word into which they had tortured my name; and "*Aidarah*," an expression signifying both *friend* and *good*. They stood motionless, waiting for a repetition of the cry, to convince themselves that their ears had not deceived them; but on my reiterating "*Totabu Aidarah*," they burst into the wildest acclamations of joy; called aloud to the shore, "*Hei Totabu, Totabu!*" and leaving their canoe to take care of itself, swam to land, incessantly repeating their exclamations of joy.

The inhabitants of Otdia, who had been observing us from behind the bushes, now that the well-known name resounded through the island, sprang from their concealment, giving vent to their rapture in frolic gestures, dances, and songs. Numbers hurried to the strand; others ran into the water as high as their hips, to be the first to welcome us. I was now generally recognised, and called Rarik, because, according to the custom prevailing here, I had sealed my friendship with that chief by an exchange of names. They also recognised Dr. Eschscholz, who had been of my former expedition, and heartily rejoiced in seeing again their beloved "*Dein Name.*" This was the name he had borne among them; because when they asked his name, and he did not understand the question, several of our people called to him "*Dein name,*" which was immediately adopted as his designation.

Four islanders lifted me from the boat, and carried me ashore, to where Lagediak awaited me with open arms, and pressed me most cordially to his bosom. The powerful tones of the muscle horn now resounded through the woods, and our friends announced the approach of Rarik. He soon appeared running at full speed towards us, and embraced me several times, endeavouring in every possible way to express his joy at our return.

Though the friends to whom I was thus restored were but poor ignorant savages, I was deeply affected by the ardour of their reception; their unsophisticated hearts beat with sincere affection towards me,—and how seldom have I felt this happy consciousness among the civilized nations of the world!

Even the women and children now made their appearance; and, among them, Rarik's loquacious mother, who with much gesticulation made me a long speech, of which I understood very little. When she had concluded, Rarik and Lagediak, each offering me an arm, led me to the house of the former.

Upon a verdant spot before it, surrounded and shaded by bread-fruit trees, young girls were busily spreading mats for Dr. Eschscholz and myself to sit on. Rarik and Lagediak seated themselves facing us, and the mother (eighty years of age) by my side, at a little distance. The other islanders formed a compact circle around us; the nearest line seating themselves, and those behind standing, to secure a better view of us. Some climbed the trees; and fathers raised their children in their arms, that they might see over the heads of the people. The women brought baskets of flowers, and decorated us with garlands; and Rarik's mother, drawing from her ears the beautiful white flower of the lily kind, so carefully cultivated here as an indispensable ornament of the female sex, did her best to fasten it into mine with strings of grass, while the people expressed their sympathy by continual cries of "*Aidarah.*" In the mean time the young girls were employed in pressing into muscle-shells the juice of the Pandanus, which they presented to us, with a sort of sweet-meat called Mogan, prepared from the same fruit; the flavour of both is very agreeable.

We were now overwhelmed with questions from all sides; to which, from our imperfect knowledge of their language, we could return but few answers. Rarik and Lagediak expressed their astonishment at the size of our ship, inquired what was become of the Rurik, and, whether their friends Timaro, Tamiso, &c. (Schischmaref and Chamisso) were still living, how they were, and why they did not accompany us.

After the first ebullition of joy at our meeting, I thought I perceived by the deportment of Rarik, that he had something on his mind; he seemed conscious of some fault, and in vain endeavoured, under friendly looks and words, to conceal a latent uneasiness. I even thought I could trace a similar feeling in his mother and Lagediak. Pained by these appearances, I asked an explanation. Rarik could no longer control his feelings, but immediately fell, like a repentant child, in tears upon my neck, without however confessing the cause of his agitation. On quitting the island eight years previously, I had appointed Kadu to the guardianship of the plants and animals we left behind, with the strongest injunctions on all the islanders to avoid injuring them, and threats of exacting a severe account on my return for any such offence. I had not yet ventured to inquire after them, fearful that the report might prove unsatisfactory, and cast a cloud over the pleasure of our meeting. It now occurred to me that Rarik must in some way have injured Kadu; perhaps he might even have put him to death. I looked sternly in

Rarik's face, while I inquired after him, but he answered me quite innocently that Kadu was well and residing on the Aur group of islands with their chief Lamari. The old mother then took up the conversation, and very diffusively related that Lamari, soon after our departure, had come hither with a fleet, and forcibly carried to Aur all the animals, plants, tools, pieces of iron,—in short, whatever we had left on the island.

Lagediak confirmed this tale, and added, that Lamari had demanded of every islander, under pain of death, the last piece of iron in his possession. Kadu, he said, soon after our departure, had married a handsome girl, the daughter or relation of the chief of Ormed; had been raised to the dignity of a Tamon-ellip, or great-commander, by Lamari; and having freely made over the half of his treasures to this personage, (a step which I had myself advised,) had been permitted to retain peaceable possession of the remainder. It was also by his own desire that Lamari had removed him to Aur, where he continued his superintendence of the plants and animals. Kadu had commissioned Lagediak to relate all these circumstances to me, with a request that I would visit him at Aur; an invitation which with regret I was prevented accepting by the large size of my ship.

I was glad however that Kadu had settled in Aur, as I hoped that the animals and plants with which I had enriched these islands would flourish under his care; and I learnt from Rarik that when he was a short time before in Aur, on a visit to his father, they had propagated, and were doing well. Swine and goats already formed part of their festival provisions, and Rarik had himself partaken of such a feast. I rejoiced in this information, and in the promise it afforded, that through my means the time may be approaching when the barbarous custom of sacrificing the third or fourth child of every marriage, from fear of famine, may wholly cease.

The cat was the only animal of those I had left at Otdia which remained there; and it was no longer of the domestic species; it had become very numerous and entirely wild, but as yet had occasioned no sensible diminution in the number of rats. It may be hoped, however, that as the cats have no other food, those voracious pests of the gardens may at length be exterminated. These cats, under the influence of a strange climate, and in an undomesticated state, may perhaps undergo some change of properties and habits, by which naturalists, always well pleased to enlarge their zoological lists, may be led to consider them as an unknown species of tiger. To obviate this error, I advertise such gentry beforehand, that the animal in question is absolutely nothing more than the ordinary European household cat.

Of the plants which we had introduced to the Radackers, the vine alone had failed. Lagediak pointed out to me the spot on which we had planted it.

It had withered, but not till, from the extreme fruitfulness of the soil, its tendrils had reached the tops of the highest trees.

I was not surprised that Kadu should have married soon after our departure a native of the island of Ormed. The girls there are particularly handsome, and we had some suspicion of an affair of the heart, from the sudden change in his previous determination to accompany us to Russia, which took place immediately after an excursion he had made with Mr. Chamisso to Ormed. Fortunately for himself, he preferred a quiet domestic life under his own beautiful sky, to tempting the severity of our Northern climate, which would probably soon have destroyed him; and fortunately for his countrymen, he remained to cultivate among them the beneficial arts of gardening and breeding of cattle.

The melancholy of Rarik still continuing after all this explanation, I again inquired the cause. He then tremblingly led me by the arm to the cocoa-tree, against which I had fastened a copper-plate, bearing the name of my ship, and the date of my discovery of the island, and denouncing severe punishment in case of its removal. It had disappeared:—how easily might Rarik and Lagediak, and the crowd of people, all equally dejected, who followed us, have excused themselves by an assertion, that Lamari, on his predatory expedition, had carried off this plate; but they were too honourable. Imploring my pardon, they candidly confessed that they had been deficient in their care of it,—that it had been stolen, and that they had been unable to discover the thief.

Rejoiced to find that their melancholy arose from no cause more serious than this, I cordially embraced my friends, while they wept for joy in my arms. Their happiness was now complete, and the multitude returned with us, shouting for joy, to Rarik's dwelling, where an *Eb*, or artless opera, was represented; the subject,—my crew of the Rurik and myself: each song celebrated one of us individually, and the praises of the whole were chanted in the concluding chorus. I regretted much that I could not understand them better. The words, *moll* (iron), *aidarah* (friend), *tamon* (commander), *oa ellip* (great boat), and Kadu's name, were frequently repeated. The Radackers preserve their traditions in these poetic representations; and as they assemble every evening to amuse themselves with dancing and singing, the children, while taking part in these innocent pleasures, learn the history of their country in the most agreeable manner, and communicate it in their turn to succeeding generations.

When the dramatic piece was concluded, and I had distributed all the little presents I had brought, I returned to my vessel, my friends promising me a visit the same day.

I now had all the boats lowered to bring ashore our tent and pendulum apparatus. The islanders received the sailors with great alacrity, brought them cocoa-nuts, helped them to disembark, and set up the tent, and appeared delighted with our intention of establishing ourselves on land.

Rarik and Lagediak were the first who visited us in the afternoon. They rowed several times in their little canoe round the ship, contemplated it very attentively, and with emotions of wonder, repeatedly exclaiming, *Erico! Erico!*—a word denoting admiration. When I met them upon deck, they forgot to salute me, stood at first riveted to the spot like statues, till an "O, o!" stretched to a minute's length, gave vent at last to their astonishment. I led them round, and showed them all that could interest them, their surprise increasing with every novelty they saw.

Lagediak inquired if the ship and all its appurtenances had been made in Russia; and on my answering in the affirmative, exclaimed, *Tamon Russia, ellip, ellip!* words which my readers will now be prepared to understand.

Lagediak soon commenced an admeasurement of the ship in all directions, with a string he had brought for this purpose: having obtained the dimensions of the ship's body, he next climbed the masts, to measure the yards and sails. My friends also expressed much surprise at the great number of men on board, and tried to count them. At the number ten, they always made a knot on a piece of string, and then began again. In comparison with the compliment of the Rurik, (only twenty men,) my present crew must have appeared extremely numerous.

A crowd of the islanders soon came on board, without the least hesitation or fear. Though very merry, and quite at home, they were all well-behaved and modest. Incessant laughter pealed from below, where these lovers of mirth had mingled with our sailors, in all sorts of tricks and jests; the different parties danced and sang alternately, each laughing heartily at the performances of the other. They exchanged embraces and presents; of the guests especially not one was empty-handed: they had brought their finest fruit, and little specimens of their handiwork; and each, with unaffected cordiality, lavished the contents of his cornucopia on a chosen friend. The setting sun gave the signal for separation, and it was obeyed amidst mutual promises of meeting again on the morrow.

Lagediak, after finishing his measurements, did not again move from my side. His desire of knowledge was boundless; nor could the explanations I was obliged to give upon the most insignificant articles satisfy his curiosity. On learning that we could stay only a few days at Otdia, he again became very sorrowful, and most earnestly pressed me to spend the remainder of my life here. He left nothing untried to procure my acquiescence in this wish: love, ambition, glory, were successively held out as lures: I should have the most beautiful woman of the islands for my wife,—should kill the tyrant and usurper Lamari, as he had killed his predecessor, and should reign in his stead Tamon of Radack. As I let him talk on without interruption, he supposed I should accede to his plans. In his joy over this offspring of his own imagination, he jumped about the cabin like a child, and, on quitting the ship, earnestly enjoined me to say nothing to Rarik of our project.

Lagediak, on visiting me again the following morning, brought me roasted fish, bread-fruit, and fresh cocoa-nuts, for breakfast: he drank coffee with me, and appeared to think it not much amiss. He brought with him his son, about thirteen or fourteen years of age, to present to me. This interesting boy appeared to inherit the disposition of his amiable father. His intelligent countenance afforded a promise, which the modesty and propriety of his conduct confirmed: he might easily have been educated for our most refined society.

Lagediak soon recurred to his yesterday's project of making me chief of Radack. He sketched the plan of its execution, and entered upon the further measures which would be requisite to give power and stability to the new government. We were first to sail to Aur and vanquish Lamari, and then to attack the hostile group of the Mediuro islands, the conquest of which would render me master of the whole chain of Radack. Animated by these valiant projects, he flourished his fist as if already in battle, till it encountered a tea-cup, which fell in a thousand fragments to the ground. His natural timidity suddenly banished the heroism into which his subject had wrought him: he feared he had done me an injury, and consequently incurred my displeasure. I re-assured him on this head, but gave him much pain by representing the impossibility of my remaining in Radack, as my duty called me elsewhere. After some minutes of silent consideration, he led his son to me, and begged I would take him with me to Russia. I was then obliged to explain to him that I should never return to Radack, and that if his son accompanied me, he must take leave of him for ever. This was too much for the father's heart; he embraced his son, and would no longer think of a separation. He was also overcome with sorrow at the idea of seeing me for the last time; and a little self-interest probably mingled in the melancholy look he cast upon a hatchet which I had given him, as he exclaimed—"I shall never get any iron again!"

I now turned the conversation on the Mediuro, and expressed a wish to know how the campaign had prospered, which Lamari, when I was last here, was about to undertake against those islands. He understood me perfectly, and taxed to the utmost his powers of pantomime to give me an account of the war, in which he had himself been engaged.

Lamari's fleet, as I understood my informant, consisted of forty vessels; and therefore, judging by the size of the boats here, the whole army could not be above four hundred strong, including the women, who, from the rear, lend assistance to the combatants by throwing stones at the enemy, and by assuming the surgeon's office. This force was collected from the whole Radack chain; the war was bloody, and lasted six whole days. Five of the enemy were slain, and Lamari gained a splendid victory with the loss of one man! The fleet returned triumphant, laden with cocoa-nuts, bread-fruit, and pandanas. Kadu had especially distinguished himself: he was armed with a sabre and lance, and wore a white shirt, and wide trowsers, which formidable attire was completed by a red cap on his head. All the hatchets, above a hundred in number, which I had given to the Radackers, and which Lamari afterwards appropriated, were fastened on long poles and distributed among the best warriors; this gave the army of Lamari a great advantage; so that I might take credit to myself for the happy issue of the campaign.

Lagediak informed me further that Lamari had also determined on an expedition to the Odia group of islands, belonging to the Ralik chain. The inhabitants of these had heard something of the treasures which the Radackers had acquired by my visit, and their rapacity being excited, had made an attack on the Kawen group of the Radack chain, without the usual declaration of war, and thus taking the inhabitants by surprise, had beaten and plundered them, and returned home laden with booty, though the Kawen people had made a valorous resistance, and killed two of the Odians without losing a man themselves. This appeared to have occurred about a year before my arrival, and the vengeance of Lamari had been hitherto delayed; the levying and provisioning an army being here a work of time. Radack is so thinly peopled that all the islands must send their quota of men, which, on account of the extension of the chain, cannot be very speedily performed. For a voyage to the Ralik chain and back, victualling for four weeks at least is necessary, as the return is against the trade-wind. The Mogan, which is principally used in these expeditions, is very nutritious, and the Radackers are very moderate, so that a small quantity suffices for their support, otherwise they could not provision their canoes for voyages of this length.

I was surprised to find Lagediak perfectly secure of the success of this undertaking, and expressed my fears that his countrymen might possibly be worsted, but he continued sanguine,—for the hatchets with which his brethren were armed, the sword, and dread-inspiring costume of Kadu, were sources of confidence which could not be abated.

During this conversation in the cabin, several islanders came on board, and the noise from below resembled that of the preceding day. Rarik had also arrived, decorated with fresh garlands of flowers, and had brought me some trifling presents. The generally-dreaded Langin, Tamon of Egmedio, presented himself to me this day, for the first time: he appeared glad to see me; but when on deck, the size of the ship, and the number of the crew, impressed him with so much alarm, that his very teeth chattered. This anguish attack continued some time, but was at length cured by our friendly deportment.

Accompanied by Rarik and Lagediak, I rowed ashore, and found Messrs. Preus and Lenz already busy with the pendulum. They were perfectly satisfied with the natives, who had behaved very well, and, except by special permission to come nearer, had kept at the appointed distance from the tent. They usually sat in a circle round the place, where the observations were made, and gazed with wonder at the astronomer who had so much business with the sun, taking him no doubt for a conjuror.

In the hours of recreation, we allowed them to come to the tent, and they always joyfully availed themselves of the permission, performing a thousand little services, which made them appear really necessary to us, yet remaining invariably so modest, gentle, and friendly, that my company declared them to be, without exception, the most amiable people on earth.

Rarik took me to his house, to witness another dramatic representation: the subject was the war on Mediuro. Women sang, or rather screamed, the deeds of the warriors; and the men in their dances endeavoured, by angry gestures and brandishing their lances, to describe the valour of the combatants. I expressed to Rarik my wish to know more of their method of warfare; he and Lagediak in consequence assembled two troops, which they opposed to each other at a short distance, as hostile armies; the first rank, in both, consisting of men, and the second of women. The former were armed with sticks instead of lances, the latter had their baskets filled with pandana seeds for stones, and their hair, instead of being as usual, tastefully bound up, hung dishevelled and wild about their heads, giving them the appearance of maniacs. Rarik placed himself at the head of one troop, and Lagediak of the other: both gave the signal for attack, by blowing their muscle horns. The adverse forces approached; but instead of the battle began a comic dance, in which the two armies emulated each other in grimaces, furious gesticulations, and a distortion of the eyes, which left only the whites visible, while the women shrieked a war-song, which, if their opponents had been lovers of harmony, would assuredly have put them to flight. The leaders on each side took no share in these violent exertions, but stood still, animating their troops by the tones of the muscle horn. When exhausted by these efforts, the horns were silent, and the armies separated by mutual consent, looking on while some of the most valiant from each side came forward to challenge with threats and abuse a champion of the enemy to single combat. This was represented by dancing and songs, and occasional movements with the hand, as if to throw the lance, which the antagonist sought to avoid by dexterously springing aside. The respective armies and their leaders animated the courage of their warriors by battle-songs, till the horns were blown again; the armies once more slowly approached each other; the champions retired into their ranks, and the battle was renewed with a prodigious noise; spears waved in the air; pandana seed flew from the delicate hands of the female warriors, over the heads of their husbands, upon the enemy, but the armies never came near enough to be really engaged. The leaders remained in front loudly blowing their horns, and sometimes giving commands. At length, by accident or design, one of Lagediak's men fell; the battle was now over, the victory decided, and the signal given for drawing off the forces. Both armies were so exhausted, that they threw themselves on the grass, and amidst laughing and merriment, gave themselves up to repose.

A large sailing-boat now put ashore, and an old man with white hair and beard was lifted from it; his shrivelled skin hung loosely over his emaciated form, and his weakness was so extreme, that he could only approach us by crawling on his hands and feet: Rarik and Lagediak went to meet and welcome him. It was my old acquaintance, Langediu, Tamon of Ormed. When our frigate lay at anchor before his island, he had not ventured, he said, to visit us, not knowing whether we were friends or foes; but when he heard that Totabu was arrived, he determined to make an effort to see me once more before his death. The old man crawled up to me and embraced me, shedding tears of joy; he talked a great deal, and spoke of Kadu being with Lamari in Aur.

On my former visit, the traces of old age were scarcely perceptible in Langediu; but in the intervening eight years they had increased rapidly; still, although his body was so weak that he could only crawl on all-fours, he retained all the faculties of his mind, all his original vivacity and good-humour, and his facetious remarks excited the merriment of the whole assembly. I have in many instances observed that at Radack, old age brings with it no particular disease, and that the mind remains unimpaired till its mortal covering sinks into the grave. A fine climate, moderate labour, and a vegetable diet, probably all contribute to produce this effect.

Langediu having intimated his wish to see the Oa ellip, I immediately rowed in my boat to the ship, followed by him in his Oa warro, or war canoe: he was much pleased with the vessel, and all that he saw, and not less so with the little presents he received; but a circumstance occurred that caused the honourable old man some chagrin: one of his attendants having concluded a friendship with the cook, took advantage of it to secrete a knife in his canoe; the cook missed the knife, and his suspicions immediately fell on his friend. His person and canoe were searched, and on the discovery of the stolen treasure the criminal confessed his fault. He trembled exceedingly, probably remembering the flogging one of his countrymen received on board the Rurik for a similar offence. As my stay was this time to be so short, I considered the flogging superfluous, and magnanimously forgave him, with a reproof, and an admonition never to steal again. Poor old Langediu was much hurt. He crawled about the ship in an agitated manner, exclaiming, *Kabuderih emo aidarah* (stealing not good), severely reprimanded, and threatened the offender,—showed him all the presents received from us, observing how much we must be shocked to be robbed, notwithstanding all our generosity. He then led him to the guns, made him remark their great number, and said, *Manih Emich, manih ni, ma,* (kill the island, kill the cocoa-trees, bread-fruit trees). Probably the old man had learned from Kadu the effect the guns would produce. After much chafing and scolding, he ordered the offender back into the canoe, and forbade him to come again on board:—not a word did the thief utter the whole time, and instantly obeyed the order to quit the vessel, but the old master could not be pacified. He frequently repeated, "*Kabuderih emo aidarah,*" and his visit afforded him no more pleasure. He took an early leave of us, requesting that we would come to him on his island.

The face of the thief appeared familiar to me; and Lagediak, in answer to my inquiries, informed me, laughing, that this was the brother of the man who had been beaten on board the Rurik. The propensity to theft appears to be a family failing. No other Radacker during our stay attempted to purloin the smallest trifle.

In the afternoon, a large boat sailed through the Lagediak Straits into the basin. I flattered myself with the arrival of some of my friends from Aur, perhaps Kadu himself; but it was the gay Labugar from Eregub, brought hither by curiosity, having seen us sail past his island.

When he heard who the strangers were, he immediately came to the ship. His joy at seeing me again was very great; but he regretted much that his friend Timaro, with whom he had exchanged names, was not of our company. The spirits of Labugar had lost during eight years none of their sprightliness; but his face looked much older, and his hair had become grey.

The fine weather induced me on the 3rd of May to visit Langediu on the island of Ormed; he received me with the greatest joy, and offered me his most costly treasures as presents. The children, grand-children, and great-grand-children of the good old man assembled round his house, and represented a dramatic piece for my amusement, in which Langediu himself played a principal part, and astonished me by the animation of his action and singing. As this was one of the best representations I have seen in

Radack, I will describe it, in the hope that my readers also will not be uninterested in it.

The number of the *dramatis personæ* was twenty-six, thirteen men and thirteen women, who seated themselves in the following order on a spot of smooth turf. Ten men sat in a semicircle, and opposite to them ten women in a semicircle also, so that by uniting the points, an entire circle would have been formed, but a space of about six feet was left at both ends, in each of which sat an old woman provided with a drum. This drum, made of the hollow trunk of a tree, is about three feet long, six inches in diameter at each end, narrowed like an hour-glass, to half that thickness in the middle. Both ends are covered with the skin of the shark: it is held under the arm, and struck with the palm of the hand. In the middle of the circle, old Langediu took his station with a handsome young woman, sitting back to back. The whole party were elegantly adorned about the head, and the females about the body also, with garlands of flowers. Outside the circle stood two men with muscle horns. The hollow tones of these horns are the signal for a chorus performed by the whole company, with violent movements of the arms and gesticulations meant to be in consonance with the words. When this ceased, a duet from the pair in the middle was accompanied by the drums and horns only; Langediu fully equalling his young companion in animation. The chorus then began again, and this alternation was repeated several times, till the young songstress whose motions had been growing more and more vehement, suddenly fell down as dead. Langediu's song then became lower and more plaintive: he bent over the body, and seemed to express the deepest sorrow; the whole circle joined in his lamentations, and the play concluded.

Deficient as was my knowledge of the language, I was still able clearly to understand the subject of this tragedy, which represented a marriage ceremony. The young girl was forced to accept of a husband whom she did not love, and preferred death to such an union. Perhaps the reason of old Langediu's playing the part of the lover might be, to give more probability to the young bride's objections and resolution.

The young females assembled here, among whom the deceased bride of Langediu soon reappeared, fresh and lively as ever, reminded me of Kadu's assertion, that the women of Ormed were the handsomest in Radack. Some of them were really very attractive, and their flowery adornments extremely becoming. These people have more taste than any other of the South Sea islanders; and the manner in which the women dress their hair, and decorate it with flowers, would have a beautiful effect even in an European ball-room. When the actors had recovered from the fatigue of their performance, dinner, which some of the females had been long preparing in the hut, was served to us. Only a few of the persons assembled enjoyed the honour of partaking our meal. Some of these were females. The ground of Langediu's hut was covered with matting, on which we sat, and the provisions were placed on clean cocoa-leaves in the middle. Every one had a cocoa-leaf for a plate. Upon the dishes were laid wooden spoons, with which the guests helped themselves,—an improvement since my former visit to Radack, when their mode was to help themselves from the dish with their hands. Langediu remarked, that the order of his table pleased me, and said *Mamuan Russia mogai* (the Russians eat so). I rejoiced in the increased civilization denoted by this more becoming mode of eating; probably introduced by Kadu, who had seen it during his stay among us. I enjoyed a still greater pleasure, when after the first course of baked and bread-fruits, came one of yams, which I had brought hither from the Sandwich Islands. At Otdia, I had been told that Lamari had carried away to Aur all the plants I had left behind. I was therefore much surprised at the sight of the yams. They perfectly supply the place of our potatoes, are wholesome and pleasant, and, if cultivated with moderate industry, are a certain resource against famine. Langediu told me, that Kadu had planted the yams on Ormed, and after dinner showed me a pretty large field very well stocked with them.

The delightful feelings with which I surveyed the new plantation may be imagined, when it is recollected, that these poor islanders, from want of means of subsistence, are compelled, assuredly with heavy hearts, to murder their own offspring, and that this yam alone is sufficient to remove so horrible a necessity. I might joyfully affirm, that through my instrumentality the distressed mother need no longer look forward to the birth of her third or fourth child with the dreadful consciousness that she endured all her pain only to deliver a sacrifice to the hand of the murderer. When she should clasp her child to her breast, and see her husband look on it with a father's tenderness, they might both remember "Totabu," and the beneficent plants which he had given them. I beg pardon for this digression, and return to our dinner.

After the yams, a number of dishes were produced, prepared from the powdered cocoa-wood, which is made with water into a thick paste, and then baked in small cakes: it has no taste at all, and cannot be very nutritious. A dessert of Mogan and Pandana juice concluded the repast. The drink was cocoa-milk, sucked from a small hole made in the nut. The conversation, in which the females, who are treated extremely well, took part, was very lively, but perfectly decorous. I wished to understand more of it: from single words, I inferred that they were speaking of the ship and of the dramatic entertainment, and should have been glad to have contributed my share to the general amusement. After I had delighted the host and the amiable company by presents of hatchets, knives, scissors, and necklaces, which latter were by no means in as great estimation here as on the Navigators' Islands, I took my leave, and returned early in the evening to the ship.

Time passed very quickly at Otdia, as it usually does when pleasantly spent; and, to the great sorrow of our friends, the day of our departure drew near. On Sunday the sailors were allowed to amuse themselves on shore; and as there were some musicians among them, they carried their instruments with them, to take leave of the islanders with a brilliant musical festival. The jubilee that ensued exceeds all description. The whole population of Otdia and the neighbouring islands assembled round our tent, and the music acted upon them like Huon's horn in Oberon. They danced and leaped about, sometimes hurrying the sailors into similar antics, and forming altogether a scene which would have provoked the most solemn philosopher to laughter. I was much pleased with observing the cordial good-will that subsisted between the natives and my crew, and with the reflection that this second visit would also leave on the minds of the Radackers an impression favourable to white men.

The females looked on at a distance during these gambols. Decorum did not allow them to mingle in them, and also restrained them from ever visiting the ship.

Among the groups I observed a crowd of children assembled round an elderly sailor, who was amusing and caressing them. He had been on duty outside the tent ever since our arrival at the islands; and as the Russians are particularly fond of children, these little creatures had grown quite sociable with him. A pretty lively little girl appeared his especial favourite. She was allowed to play him all kinds of tricks, without being reproved; and even when she pulled him by the hair, he pulled again, and seemed as much entertained as she was.

When the islanders learned the day fixed for our departure, they visited us on board in greater numbers than ever, always bringing presents with them. They spoke of parting with great sorrow, and earnestly pressed us to return soon. With respect to the presents we had recently made them, they expressed their fears that Lamari would again plunder them, when he should learn that we had been there. I therefore commissioned Lagediak, in the presence of a great number of islanders, to inform Lamari, from me, that if he should ever presume to plunder the possessor of the smallest article presented by us, whenever white men should again visit Radack, they would, without fail, take signal and severe vengeance upon him. He understood me, and promised to execute my commission.

Lagediak now seldom left me; and his grief at our approaching separation was really affecting. On the morning of the appointed day, the 6th of May, when we had begun to weigh anchor, he came in great haste in a large canoe, and brought a number of young cocoa-plants. On my inquiring for what purpose he intended them, he answered, that he wished me to plant them in Russia, in remembrance of him. I then recollected his having once asked me if cocoa-trees grew in Russia, and that I had of course replied in the negative. He had then turned the conversation on some other subject, and I thought no more of it. He had however resolved on enriching my country with this fine fruit, and had reserved for the day of our parting this last proof of his regard. I explained to him that it was far too cold in Russia for the cocoa-trees to flourish, and that for that reason I was unwilling to rob him of his plants. He mourned much over the failure of his kind intentions, packed up his plants again, and when he saw our sails spread and our departure inevitable, took leave of us like a child that is forcibly separated from beloved parents. To the rest of our friends we had bidden farewell the evening before.

We sailed through the Schischmaref straits, and then between the Otdia and Aur groups, whence we steered directly to the group Ligiep, in order to lay down correctly its eastern coasts, for which, in my former voyage, circumstances had been unfavourable. On the following day we reached the southern edge of this group, and sailed near enough to see from thence clear over to the northern. We then proceeded westward, keeping always near enough to the islands to distinguish objects upon them with the naked eye. I now plainly perceived that the course I had taken in the Rurik had prevented my seeing the whole of this group; and the result is, that it appears on the accompanying map, according to our present correct survey, half as large again as I had before represented it.

The inhabitants of Ligiep, on seeing the ship, directly put out to sea from between the reefs, in a crowd of sailing canoes, to follow us, but were too timid to come within cannon-shot. We lay-to, when they also took in their sails, but contented themselves with contemplating us from a safe distance; and as the favourable weather would not permit us to waste more time, we continued our voyage without making farther attempts to entice them to the ship.

On the north-west, of the group Ligiep we found several larger islands, which, being covered with fine cocoa-trees, induced the supposition that they may be more thickly peopled.

We also found, as is shown upon the map, two broad entrances to the inland sea round which this group is scattered, which, after a very accurate examination, appeared perfectly safe and convenient for the passage of the largest ship of the line, since, according to their direction, it is possible, by help of the trade-wind, to sail in and out without tacking. There seems no doubt that the interior of this group offers the best anchorage; and should any navigator wish to put into Radack, I recommend this harbour to him as the most commodious.

At noon the north-west point of the Ligiep group lay about a mile off us due east, and we found by a close observation the latitude to be 10° 3' 40" North, and the longitude 190° 58' 3".

Directly after this observation, I had all sail set, and steered with a fresh wind to the north-west, in the hope of falling in with the group Ralik.

As darkness came on, we again took in most of the sails, and endeavoured to keep the vessel during the night as much as possible on the same spot. With break of day we continued our voyage; but the weather, hitherto so fine, now became very gloomy. The heavy rain permitted us only to see to a short distance; and as no hope of improvement appeared, I gave up the idea of visiting Ralik, and bent my course direct for Kamtschatka.

We often thought and conversed upon the interesting inhabitants of Radack, of whom we had for ever taken leave. Since this chain lies far out of the course usually pursued by navigators in the South Sea, it will not soon be visited again, and may in course of time be entirely forgotten. Whether this will be for their benefit or their misfortune, he who rules the destinies of man can alone foresee.

It is certain that the Radack chain has been peopled much later than most of the South Sea islands; but whence, and at what period, is quite unknown. If a conjecture may be hazarded, it would be, that the inhabitants owe their origin to the Corolinas. They have no tradition on the subject. Their language is quite different from all the Polynesian dialects, and appears of more recent formation. Whence have these people derived characters so much superior to those of other South Sea islanders, many of whom, enjoying as fine a climate, and a more bountiful soil, resemble beasts of prey? I attribute this in some measure to the superior purity of manners among the females. Experience teaches us, that wherever that sex is held in its due estimation, morals are proportionably refined.

To be thus esteemed, woman must resist the attacks of licentiousness. When she associates virtue with her other attractions, she will soon obtain an influence over the most savage of the other sex; and thus have the females of Radack contributed to form the amiable character of their countrymen.

Other fortunate circumstances may have combined with this, to which the ante-christian Tahaitians were certainly not indebted. It is justice, however, to assert here, that, upon perfect conviction, I give a decided preference to the Radackers over the inhabitants of Tahaiti.

END OF THE FIRST VOLUME.

FOOTNOTES:

Namely English miles, of which sixty go to a degree, and four to a German mile. Whenever, in this Voyage, miles are mentioned, English miles are to be understood.

The longitude is always calculated from Greenwich, in this work.

"Formidable is man in his misguided zeal."

The measurement given is two Russian wersts, of which one hundred and four and a half make a degree, or, as nearly as possible, one and a half make an English mile. The exact circumference therefore of the lake, as given, is one mile and one third.

Upon the maps, Lioné and Fanfouné; the termination in *h* denotes, in the Polynesian language, the accent upon the last syllable; as in the Tahaitian name Pomareh.

This group must not be confounded with *Otdia* where we were at this time.

Lightning Source UK Ltd.
Milton Keynes UK
UKHW010745271222
414464UK00004B/303